CAREERS IN

AIRLINES AND AIRPORTS

Verité Reily Collins

KOGAN
PAGE

First published in 2002

Kogan Page Limited
120 Pentonville Road
London N1 9JN
UK

British Library Cataloguing in Publication Data

A CIP record for this book is available from the British Library.

ISBN 0 7494 3702 2

Typeset by Jean Cussons Typesetting, Diss, Norfolk
Printed and bound in Great Britain by Clays Ltd, St Ives plc

Contents

About the author

Verité Reily Collins worked for an airline, and flies on them constantly in her work. In training she was the first individual to be awarded ABTA's Seal of Approval, and has sat on NVQ development committees since their start. She was European Correspondent for *Onboard Services Magazine* (the US's top airline professionals' magazine), and now writes for *Headstart, Airports International, Airline World, In-flight Entertainment*, etc and provides articles on working in the industry for the *Sunday Express, Careerscope*, etc.

Acknowledgements

With many thanks to all the people who shared their experiences and helped on the book, including Public Relations at Norwich Airport, Margaret Pecnik of BALPA, Jessica de Ridder of IATA, Ann Watson of EAL, Daniel Cooke, KLM and KLM uk's press offices, Anne Kavanagh PR, Bob Lake of BA who was an excellent teacher, and helpful friend whenever luggage went missing, Ann Watson of EAL EMTA Awards, and John Clare of the *Daily Telegraph* for permission to quote.

1 Introduction

Working in the aviation world is exciting, interesting and very hard work. Although over 100,000 people work in this industry in Britain, plus another 250,000 in support services, it is often difficult to find information about jobs, and even more difficult to find employment. It can seem like a closed shop to someone wanting to find work in the industry. However, IATA says 'demand for air transport doubles about every 10 years', so the jobs are there. This book tells you what qualifications you need and how to find different types of work.

In the century since the Wright Brothers flew the first powered aeroplane, air travel has extended around the world. Today, hundreds of companies battle to attract holidaymakers and business travellers flying to an increasing number of destinations. Every aircraft that takes off needs support services, administration and flight crew.

You would think the Web would make it easier to find a job. But Web sites can sometimes be off-putting, and often don't answer your questions. So, in this book we aim to give an insight into what jobs are really like, and how to find them. The Case Studies are one person's experiences – although most employees have similar experiences. We have also quoted some salaries: these change rapidly, so we have only printed those that were quoted within one month of writing the book.

History

It all started on 17 December 1903, when Orville Wright took to the air at Kill Devil Hill, near Kitty Hawk in North Carolina. The first flight took 12 seconds to travel 120 ft, but by that evening his brother Wilbur, when his turn came, had flown 850 ft in almost a minute. The demands of World War I helped the development of aircraft, and by 7 October 1919 KLM had flown its first commercial flight. The airline continues to operate under the same name to this day and is the world's oldest airline company. Why KLM? It stands for Koninklijke Luchvaart Maatschappij (Royal Dutch Airlines).

KLM's first scheduled flight, on 17 May 1920, connected Croydon (London) with Amsterdam. A De Havilland DH-16 took off with two journalists, a bundle of newspapers and a message from the Lord Mayor of London. By the end of the year, the company had carried 345 passengers, 22 tons of cargo and 3 tons of mail. This innovation had become a success.

The airline operated its first intercontinental flight to Indonesia in October 1924. Regular scheduled flights to the Far East began in 1929 and during World War II KLM moved base to England. In 1945, its homebase, Amsterdam Airport Schiphol, had to be reconstructed from zero and Albert Plesman, who had founded and led KLM from the beginning, threw himself into this task with the same energy he had applied to the pre-war company. By the autumn of 1945 Far Eastern services had recommenced and in May 1946 KLM was the first continental European airline to open transatlantic services to the USA.

In the 1930s, Britain's Imperial Airways forged links with the countries of the then British Empire (later the Commonwealth), the world's largest 'group' of countries. These countries needed to do business with each other, and London. So Imperial developed routes across the globe, all returning to their hub, or 'mother' airport at Croydon. Small airlines belonging to different countries fed into the system. These countries may not have been in the British Empire, but it made sense to use

Imperial's routes so they could feed passengers into a worldwide system.

Such a complicated spider's web of routes developed that today it would be impossible to disband them and start again. When Heathrow became the centre of this spider's web and the world's busiest airport (the biggest is Chicago's O'Hare), the world's airlines had to time departures for Heathrow's convenience. Heathrow doesn't allow more than a small amount of night flights, which means that flights from Asia often have to start in the middle of their night.

At the end of World War II, there were many surplus planes. It didn't take long for entrepreneurs to buy these and start flying scheduled and charter routes. Sadly, a very large percentage went bankrupt, principally because the bosses were long on enthusiasm but short on financial knowledge. But eventually the business sorted itself out, and today most airlines are headed for growth with the introduction of new routes, loyalty programmes such as Air Miles, new airports and, of course, aircraft that may in the not so distant future carry thousands rather than hundreds of passengers.

The only factor holding back growth in Britain is lack of airport capacity. When Heathrow was built just over 50 years ago, the planners believed that air travel would never be for the masses. So only a narrow access tunnel was built, which is constantly jammed with traffic, causing BAA to invest heavily in the Heathrow Express train link between Paddington Station and the airport.

Today, Continental airports such as Frankfurt, Schiphol, Charles de Gaulle, etc are snapping at Heathrow's heels. They have room to expand, and for the past 10 years Schiphol has mounted an aggressive campaign to persuade British people living outside London and flying long haul that it is quicker to fly to the Netherlands to change planes, rather than put up with congestion at Heathrow. Frankfurt makes a big play on the fact that their terminals are nearer so transfers are quicker – hmmm! But it offers 277 destinations, more than any other European airport.

KLM's marketing plan is based on attracting more passengers

from neighbouring countries, as its 'Dutch home market is not large enough to sustain a major international carrier'.

Airport rivalry alerts potential passengers to what is on offer, so eventually this provides more jobs! Although Heathrow wants to expand from its current 60 million-plus passengers a year, most passengers are probably happy that London has five airports to choose from (Heathrow, Gatwick, London City, Stansted and Luton) and will choose the nearest.

Looking at the past history of the airline industry and the endless possibilities for the future, it is easy to see why working in aviation is one of the most exciting areas of the travel industry. On the ground, behind the scenes or with direct customer contact, opportunities are endless. The commercial aviation industry needs staff with a wide range of skills.

The industry today

The majority of air travellers fly economy or tourist class (known as coach class in the United States). Once all airlines flew the same seat configuration, and passengers were just pleased to get to their destination faster than previous generations. Now, with aircraft fitted out to take four classes: first, business, premium and economy (different airlines have different names), complaints are soaring. *Newsweek Magazine* says passengers are part of the problem, demanding cheaper and cheaper fares. 'If passengers want airlines to treat them better, they're going to have to reward those carriers that do.' Instead of booking on low-cost, no-frills airlines, they should be prepared to pay a bit more and travel on airlines with extra comfort.

All is not gloom. High-revenue business and first-class passengers prepared to pay more are increasing at a phenomenal rate. Recent figures from American Express show airline revenue from premium-class fares is increasing – albeit slowly due to the after effects of September 11th 2001. Now, companies are alarmed at the rise in airline fares, and accountants are constantly trying to persuade executives to downgrade. So, as Matthew Davis of American Express says, 'canny airlines have jumped to the rescue by... offering the business traveller a broader range of options', such as British Airways' superb upgraded club class product as an alternative to first class.

Video conferencing was supposed stop many business flights, but seems to have had the opposite effect. Companies have a video call to set up their meeting, then fly to the meeting.

All this extra high-income revenue travel means that not only are more cabin crew needed to supply upgraded services, but also more support staff such as VIP Lounge receptionists, more check-in staff, dedicated porters, limousine drivers, etc.

The general public sees working for an airline as a glamorous job, but cabin crew have to combine working as a flying waiter or waitress, mobile shop assistant, clearing up if someone is sick, handling air rage, etc. Then when you arrive at your destination, some airlines now expect crew to clean out the aircraft. You don't often get a stopover in a glamorous destination – particularly when you start. It's usually a turn-round within the hour, and back on your feet again, handing out food and drink on the returning flight.

Airports

It is not only airlines that are making money from air travellers; airports make a profit by charging planes every time they land or take off, and the biggest success story has been airport shopping. When the British Airports Authority (BAA) was privatized it realized the tremendous retailing asset contained at airports, with a captive audience. Now many airports make as much profit on retail business as they do on landing fees, etc. Consequently, airport retailers are major employers worldwide.

Airport retail is helped by the escalating problem of delays to incoming aircraft. You might imagine that spare aircraft are parked in a hanger to be used if one goes u/s (unserviceable). The reality is that unless airlines keep aircraft flying – actually in the air – at least 16 out of 24 hours, it is difficult to make a profit.

Delays

Recently, the Association of European Airlines said that the number of delayed flights within Europe had doubled in the past decade. Now it is estimated one in five charter flights will be delayed by an hour or more. In the same period, demand for air travel between Britain and the Continent has increased by around 80 per cent – with charter airlines carrying around 35 million passengers a year. And this is expected to rise.

All sorts of problems can cause an aircraft to arrive late, and with less than an hour for most flights to 'turn around' – disembark passengers, clean the aircraft, load on food and drink, passengers and luggage – there is a full chance it will leave late.

Problems include: bad weather; a 'technical' (engineering fault) with the plane; a passenger who checks in their baggage, then spends too long shopping and arrives late on the aircraft; a strike by one of the services, be it baggage handlers or coach drivers. All have a knock-on effect around the world.

Delays have meant passengers taking a longer look at regional airports. Their image used to be one of down-market and cheap airports for charters; scheduled flights took off from glamorous international airports. Today, when these airports can advertise and deliver a 10-minute check-in time from arrival to boarding the aircraft, business flyers are sitting up and taking notice. Regional airports are increasing their through-put, and clever marketing by European airports such as Frankfurt and Schiphol offers flights from these gateways, with a short transfer time onto intercontinental flights. For example, passengers from Liverpool, instead of taking a train to Reading, transferring to a coach and then flying from Heathrow, are now driving direct to their local airport, flying to Amsterdam and transiting onto an intercontinental flight. Much quicker. And the duty-free shops at Amsterdam are delighted!

Air traffic control

Other problems come with overcrowded skies. Up above you are 'skylanes' in which planes travel from east to west and north to south, with corresponding lanes underneath/above for traffic going from west to east and south to north. Like a giant 3D noughts and crosses game. But this time the game is played with people's lives. For safety, aircraft keep a certain distance from the one in front and the one behind, plus there is a buffer expanse of sky above and below. These spaces are controlled by air traffic controllers (ATCs) across the world, who have the task of slotting aircraft into the appropriate 'skylane' and monitoring progress.

One good thing is that ATCs talk to each other in English: even in the remotest regions of the earth, the ATC language is our mother tongue. When the Oxford Delegacy Examination Board asked a senior examiner to produce an American and Australian version of the Tourism English Proficiency Exam, she refused, citing that the exam would be taken by airline pilots and ATCs who were taught basic English – not other versions. She lost her job, but shortly afterwards a plane crashed because the pilot and ATC had not been able to understand each other.

Apart from slotting in when they take to the skies, aircraft have to be parked on the ground, and the world's airports are fast running out of space. Heathrow is desperate to build a fifth terminal, and Schiphol is talking about constructing an airport out in the North Sea. This all means yet more jobs.

Working in the industry

Before you can even start trying to find employment, you have to sort out a maze of employers, and plan how to survive the dreaded interview. Airlines such as United Airlines, All Nippon, American Airlines, etc, recruit in Britain, as do Cathay Pacific, Japan Airlines, Emirates, Gulf Air, etc. British Airways is one of the largest airlines, and many charter airlines, such as Britannia, Monarch, Air 2000, etc, are major employers. British Midland now has rights to fly across the Atlantic and low-cost airlines constantly need more staff.

However, salaries, especially on 'no-frills' airlines, are much less than you might expect. How do you think airlines offer such low fares? Although allowances can be generous for shift work, the lucrative shifts generally go to people who have worked longest for the company.

At airports, the big success story is retail shopping – BAA and Nuance have contracts all over the world to operate airports and duty-free shops, and recruit staff working at their outlets in Britain for these glamorous posts. The jobs are there – but can you offer what employers want?

2 Working for airlines

Employers and types of work

British airline companies are among the largest, most efficient and most profitable in the world. They gained this reputation by severe trimming both in costs and in personnel. So don't expect an easy job.

There are two sides to work in this sector. First, flight operations in front of the public. The public face of airlines comes from the crew: pilots, cabin and check-in staff. Second, administration behind-the-scenes: reservations, sales and marketing, information technology (IT), business planning and development. Depending on the size of the airline, several jobs could be combined, or there could be a whole department handling one job's functions.

The two 'streams' work in parallel, but it isn't often that one swaps over to the other. If this happens, usually a crew member takes a senior position training pilots or cabin crew.

Most airlines run a graduate programme, but vacancies will depend on time of year (obviously) and on economic factors. If you are interested in an airline career, many airlines run work placement schemes, which are usually advertised on their Web sites. It's worth asking around, especially if there is a small airline near your home that might not have many applicants.

Then there are cargo departments. If you are interested in logistics, this could be the place to go.

Jobs at the airlines

Arrivals service duty manager

One of my favourite people at Heathrow Airport is Bob Lake, now an arrivals service duty manager for British Airways. He is the person in charge of 'lost and found' or, as airlines like to call it, 'mis-routed luggage'. If a piece of luggage is lost, Bob knows where to find it – stuck in Alaska or behind an office filing cabinet. Today, thanks to the computer, his job is probably easier in the luggage department, but problems are always there for arriving passengers.

Tip!

Bob wanted to work for an airline. He says 'I took an office job in accounts. Take whatever jobs are going as there are always lots of internal opportunities.'

Cabin crew support/crewing operations

To get an aircraft into the air needs a crew of pilots and cabin staff. Charged with getting the crew onto the aircraft are cabin crew support. They collate the paperwork and information that pilots need to fly an aircraft; from plans of the airport/s en route, plus all diversion airports, weather reports, etc. They work out fuel required, organize crew rosters, book overnight hotels if needed, check crew are up-to-date with training, arrange courses, amend aircraft flight manuals and emergency checklists, and a whole lot more.

They work out crew rosters (taking account of preferences, which could be 'I must have that day off for my kid's sports day' to 'I am getting married on…'). When dealing with several thousand staff, this can be a nightmare! They also have to ensure that passports, inoculations and vaccinations are up-to-date, otherwise a crew member may be refused entry to a country. The number of crew needed depends on the aircraft type, and the support team has to ensure that crew are qualified to fly on the type of aircraft. This is important – different aircraft have emergency exits positioned in different sections of the airframe, and the consequences don't bear thinking about if there is a fire and a crew member is searching for the exit door in the wrong area.

Salary

A tactical flight planning officer earns £15,784 plus shift allowances.

Call centres

Call centres handle the all-important airline ticket sales, or telephone sales. Call centres for companies such as BA, British Midland, etc are often based in large complexes on industrial estates in Manchester, Glasgow, Newcastle-upon-Tyne, etc, well away from airports and cities, where space is cheaper. Staff deal with travel agents and the general public, making reservations, answering queries, quoting fares and issuing tickets. If you are disabled, particularly wheelchair-bound, this is an area that might well give you employment where you can use your skills.

If you speak a language fluently, many US airlines now employ staff in Britain in call centres to handle telephone book-ings Europe-wide. For example, someone in Spain phones to book a flight from Madrid to New York. They call a local tele-phone number in their country, which automatically re-routes them to an office in Britain (the caller only pays for a local call, with the airline picking up the difference). In Britain they are answered by someone speaking fluent Spanish, and probably never know where their booking is handled. Computers linked with Spain, Germany, France, etc will automatically issue the ticket. Ain't science wonderful!

Tip!

Don't believe the recruitment agency that says working for an airline's call centre selling airline tickets means 'you will be able to transfer over to cabin crew'. Believe that...!!

Cargo

Most major airlines have a cargo department using spare space in the giant holds underneath seating cabins. And there are airlines that only handle cargo, such as DHL and Federal Express. Most major airlines such as Finnair, KLM, JAL etc, have their own cargo divisions. BA World Cargo is the world's fifth largest international cargo carrier, carrying a million tons of freight, mail and courier shipments a year with a team of 2,900 working for this section. Their base, Ascentis, is the size of six football pitches, and one of the largest automated freight depots in the world.

Carrying perishable food such as strawberries and other fruit is one of the most profitable cargo operations, and it all started when American airline TWA wanted to utilize spare space to make a bit of money. Persuading Florida growers it would pay them to ship their citrus and other fruit to Europe, from this germ of an idea spread the giant industry that carries food from countries around the world to markets eager for exotic produce.

Carrying racehorses around the world to top courses is another profitable section, and whenever there is a major earthquake, hurricane, flood or other disaster the aid agencies such as the Red Cross will be booking the giant Russian Antenov 124, the world's largest cargo carrier, to carry aid swiftly to where it is most needed.

Cargo needs marketing, finance, IT and business planning staff as well as pilots to fly cargo planes.

Cargo call centre agent

When a call comes in to ship something by air, it will be handled by an agent.

Case Study

Shipping a piano *from London to Carnegie Hall, New York.*

One typical problem handled by a BA call centre agent came through from a well-known concert promoter in London one Thursday morning. They had put together a concert in New York's famed Carnegie Hall, and their temperamental artiste suddenly wanted the Steinway piano he played on last time he gave a concert in London. Never mind that the concert is due to take place on Friday evening – when artistes of his stature demand something, they get it. It needs to be flown in urgently; a call to BA sets everything in train. The agent checks that the piano will be properly crated, checks weight and size, then reserves space in a cargo plane flying out that night.

At Heathrow the piano is handled by a customs service agent at Carrus, BA's new business centre, where the agent issues bar-code documentation and checks customs forms are in order. Then the lorry carrying the piano drives round to the front of Ascentis, where the airline takes over. Using sophisticated automated loading/unloading equipment, the Steinway is soon on its way through a range of security and tracking systems.

Behind the scenes, flight planners are checking that day's loads, carefully balancing the cargo to make sure freight is evenly distributed. By 10 pm the piano is in the hold of a 747 taxiing down the runway to New York.

Friday morning the piano is being unloaded at JFK Airport. After customs clearance it is sent to Carnegie Hall, unpacked, tuned, and the artiste is playing it during final rehearsal – a happy man!]

Despatcher

The despatcher is the key figure before any aircraft departs from an airport. About 90 minutes before the ETD (estimated time of departure) a very fit person reports for duty at the gate. Fit, because he or she will have a lot of running around to do in the next hour and a half. Despatchers take pride in ensuring 'their' aircraft leaves on time. They monitor the service and provisioning vehicles buzzing around on the tarmac beneath the aircraft; check that passengers have been alerted by an announcement to prepare for boarding; ensure that engineers have completed their checks; oversee food and drink coming on board, ensuring that the correct number of meals and any special orders are there; and ensure that cargo has been loaded, baggage is progressing smoothly, fuel has been taken on board, and the crew have arrived – all the time running up and down ladders and stairs. Once everything is OK on board, it's a quick dash to the departure lounge to oversee boarding – checking passes and tickets and ensuring that special-needs passengers are alright.

They are also responsible for compiling data regarding the correct weight and balance of an aircraft, to ensure its weight is correctly distributed and loaded, so it is safe to fly. Generally this is done on a sophisticated computer, so IT skills are necessary, but it can also be done manually, so your maths must be good.

With everyone either on board or waiting in the departure lounge, it's a sprint back on board, up another staircase to hand the captain the load sheet, which gives details of everything the aircraft is carrying, from passengers to fuel. Cargo and baggage is marked accurately so the captain knows where the centre of gravity is on the aircraft – vital for a smooth take-off and to make maximum effective use of the fuel on board. Then the tractor tug arrives to tow out the aircraft, another dash to make sure all the hold doors are secure, then time for a wave to send the aircraft on its way, before the despatcher starts the process for the next flight.

Finance

Airlines are in business to make a profit. Revenue and pricing have to ensure that an aircraft goes out with as many full seats as possible; once the flight takes off, it is impossible to obtain revenue from an empty seat. So an airline has to carefully balance offering cheap seats to a consolidator or the general public, with the chance that someone may come along at the last minute and pay top price. Analysts are crucial to profitable operations, and an airline needs to know how things as diverse as oil prices and food costs will affect its accounts. There will be liaison between the airline and IATA (the International Air Transport Association), to ensure that revenue from legs sold by travel agents or other airlines is credited to the airline as quickly as possible.

Ground operations staff

On the ground there are a whole range of jobs for staff who check aircraft before passengers arrive, order fuel, liaise with air traffic control over slot allocations (take-off times), etc. The main working area is the apron, so you could be outside in all weathers. You start as an apron hand:

◆ loading and unloading aircraft with baggage, freight, ballast mail etc;
◆ driving ground operations equipment for loading and unloading;
◆ marshalling aircraft into parking positions;
◆ overseeing toilet and water services.

In-flight entertainment (IFE)

Someone has to do it – review and choose films and music. Distribution companies usually have the task of choosing and vetting films, etc.

IT (information technology)

You would have to search to find a department that didn't rely on IT. Tracking down a spare part; planning for optimum use of fuel; checking in passengers – all this and more depends on IT. BA has over 2,000 IT professionals working as solutions managers, technical consultants/architects, analysts, systems management back-up, Unix senior technical analysts, information management developers, systems developers and capacity management team leaders. Most airlines recruit both experienced staff with a minimum of one year's experience, and graduates. Airlines ask for good knowledge of any of the following: HTML, JAVA, SQL, SSDM, Oracle, VB, MVS, OS2, TPF, DB2, PL1, Lotus NV, Business Objects or Microsoft Com, and if possible, experience of analysis, rational rose, systems modelling, business modelling, SSADM systems design or database design.

Salary

An e-commerce co-ordinator will earn £15,756–17,723 pa.

Lounges

Many airlines offer first- and business-class passengers a dedi-cated lounge, away from the bustle of the departure area. Inside the lounge it is calm and peaceful, guests can help themselves to a drink or snack, make last-minute telephone calls, and even have a shower or nap in some. These lounges are staffed by receptionists with good host or hostess skills – not as in a night club, but in the old-fashioned way of making people feel welcome in your home.

The latest idea is to provide 'arrivals lounges' for premium-rate passengers to use after they have arrived – particularly after a long-haul flight. As you stumble off your overnight flight, you go to the airline's lounge, take a shower, give your suit to the valet to press, and have breakfast.

Most airports have business centres, offering day offices and conference facilities; using airports for business meetings is extremely popular. These centres need staff who have good telephone and secretarial skills, and know how to operate conference aids.

Many airports, such as Luton, have a dedicated area for chil-dren, where they can let off steam, play games, bounce around and generally make a noise without disturbing other passengers. NNEB or NVQ in Childcare Skills is needed. There are also lounges dedicated to young flyers, such as BA's Skyflyers. These kids travel the world back and forth, flying out to parents for the holidays, and back to school. Probably some of the most sophisticated flyers are to be found here – they know every-thing about flying and are very independent. You have to be cool to work here.

Loyalty programmes

The giant Pitney Bowes corporation has carried out research into what motivates people. According to their Vice President,

Meredith Fischer, 'airline loyalty programmes are amongst the best'. All the major airlines offer 'perks' for customer loyalty, such as special lounges needing receptionists.

Another loyalty programme is 'Air Miles'. The company was set up and founded as the brainchild of three entrepreneurs in the UK around 13 years ago. They then sold the concept to British Airways, set up a company called Loyalty Management International and took the idea out to Spain, the Netherlands and Canada.

Customers build up Air Miles when they fly with British Airways, take petrol at a Shell station, use certain car parks, send flowers with Flying Flowers, use NatWest cards or even buy a washing machine. These 'miles' can then be used for holidays, etc. They are very popular with executives, encouraging loyalty amongst frequent customers who will go out of their way to fly by the airline whose 'miles' they collect, even if there are more convenient flight times.

The company has bases in Warrington, Birchwood and Gatwick, and employs account managers, administration staff, call centre staff, customer services staff, etc. Recruitment administrator Sue Fenner says 'peak time for recruitment is April–October. On top of your salary you receive 50 air miles when you join, another 250 when you have finished your probationary period, 250 on each birthday plus rewards of miles for sales, etc.' See www.talent.airmiles.co.uk.

Marketing

Although more people are travelling by air, new airlines start up constantly. So how does one airline encourage passengers to fly with them rather than with a rival?

This is a job for 'marketing'. Sometimes the department is in-house (belonging to the company); sometimes an airline will go out to an advertising agency to handle their advertising and marketing, and some airlines employ a mix of both roles.

Encouraging passengers to fly *your* airline is a fascinating career. When scheduled airlines first started, only the rich could afford to fly, but as prices came down, more and more passengers came along. First airline ads emphasized the glamour and excitement of flying, and to some extent this is still the focus of many advertisements. Before World War II, there was glamour. It took three days to fly to Egypt, and on the way you sat in individual seats, were served delicious meals and had a chance to meet and talk to fellow passengers, especially when you landed to stay in a top hotel overnight. After the War, when Dakotas and other aircraft became readily available, the concept was created of cramming as many seats into an aircraft as possible. Flights were quicker, and as far as glamour was concerned, this disappeared – except in the minds of the advertising copywriters.

Lufthansa caused much interest with a series of ads on the reality behind the myth. Cartoons debunked every copywriter's cliché, from 'our gourmet cuisine' to 'stretch out and sleep away the miles'. One cartoon showed in hilarious detail 'the early morning queue for the loos'.

Unfortunately other airlines objected – so the ads ceased. In their place came the brilliant Saatchi and Saatchi inspired strapline: 'The World's Favourite Airline'. Actually, BA has never been awarded this accolade – except by their advertising agency – but the general public accepted this statement at face value. BA said it was justified because they were carrying more international passengers than any other airline.

However, today travellers are much more sophisticated. Businesspeople need reassurance that flights are going to be on time, holidaymakers know flying is going to be boring, and want something to entertain them in-flight. So marketing departments get together to think up new concepts. At the beginning of the 1990s, every airline wanted in-flight entertainment: seat-back videos and telephones at every seat. Swissair pioneered this concept with incredibly difficult technology using satellites, allowing passengers to contact people on the ground by telephone. Every seat was fitted with a telephone, which cost Swissair a fortune.

So Swissair's rivals had to follow. However, marketing departments were made to think seriously about the costs when, in a very well-publicized incident, some members of the England football squad trashed airline seats on the way back from Hong Kong. Not only did the airline have to pacify fellow passengers, but it also meant that seats were unsaleable on a high-revenue route, until the aircraft could return to base and fit new ones. Seat-back telephones have now been removed from most seats – there may be one or two telephones in a cabin – most passengers prefer to use their own mobiles when they land.

Market research constantly says that what passengers want most is legroom. But, the more seats an airline crams in, the higher the revenue. Business-class passengers pay up to 12 times more than an economy passenger, so they get the extra room. Economy-class passengers may say they want legroom, but they won't pay extra.

It took several well-publicized deaths from DVT (deep vein thrombosis), where lack of legroom could have been a contributory factor, for passengers and airlines to think again about the cost of extra space. Now it is a race between the world's airlines to take out seats and give passengers what they want.

Case Study

American Airlines *provide extra legroom.*

American Airlines were probably the first major airline to take out seats. Their public relations team issued the following press release, which was widely quoted around the world:

American Airlines provides extra legroom for every economy passenger
Transatlantic passengers asked for more legroom in the economy cabin and it has now arrived, as American Airlines' newly-configured *More Room in Coach* aircraft appear in the UK. Passengers flying with American from London Heathrow, London Gatwick, Birmingham, Manchester and Glasgow are starting to experience up to 36 inches of legroom at every economy seat.
  American is currently removing more than 7,200 seats from economy cabins. To date, 96 per cent of American's fleet has had an average of two rows of seats taken from each aircraft, increasing seat pitch from the industry standard of 31–32 inches to 34–35 inches.
  'Few initiatives in the history of our airline have produced as much

positive feedback among customers, employees and industry observers as the More Room In Coach campaign,' said Jon Snook, American's managing director of European sales. 'Feedback from corporate customers, travel agents, tour operators and passengers in Europe overwhelmingly endorses our plan to give passengers on every flight more room and a more comfortable seat.'

One passenger commented 'It's incredible', and another said 'It's a big reason to try harder to go American Airlines'. That's just what the airline wants to hear!

Newsweek Magazine says this cost American $70 million. Meanwhile BA has been castigated by passengers and the media for fitting 10 seats across in a 3–4–3 configuration in its 777s, flying to the Caribbean under the AML banner. BA has now decided to reduce seating density to bring these aircraft into line with others.

Watch this space – as they say. And if you are interested in working in marketing, read the Kogan Page book *Careers in Marketing, Advertising and Public Relations.*

Office staff

Office staff tend to work more regular hours but in emergencies may be needed to provide telephone cover during evenings and weekends to support staff at the airport. Some airlines offer a general training scheme that covers accounts, cargo, sales and marketing, reservations, passenger services, computer operations and personnel (human resources).

Operations

Sometimes likened to a spider sitting in the middle of its web, it is this department's job to monitor comings and goings of aircraft, troubleshooting when things go wrong. It is thanks to hard work by operations staff that more aircraft aren't delayed. Whenever an airline's aircraft are in the air, operations are working, ensuring the right aircraft is in the right place at the right time. If you like a quiet life – this isn't the job for you!

When things are going smoothly Ops doesn't have much to do – a rare occasion! But at the hint of bad weather, strikes, terrorism alerts or a thousand other problems they swing into action.

Case Study

Operations *in action.*

A Hurricane out in the Gulf of Mexico suddenly takes an unexpected sweep north, and Florida is about to be hit by the storm. Passengers decide to cut short their holiday and fly home early; it is peak season, so most flights are full. Thinking on their feet, Ops realize that their Caribbean flights are less than half full, so diverting one plane empty to Florida takes care of the extra passengers there, whilst two Caribbean destinations are amalgamated with one aircraft picking up at both desti- nations. All that remains to be done is to pacify those passengers who will be delayed.

Whilst this is going on, an aircraft becomes u/s (unserviceable) before take-off in Bangkok. An engineer is contacted, who talks the main- tenance crew in Bangkok through the problem, suggesting solutions. By the time the problem is fixed, the crew won't be able to take off on the long haul back to London, as they will be out of hours. Ops realized this would happen, and whilst passengers were being pacified with meals during the wait, they found a crew in Hong Kong. However, no commer- cial flight was available to bring them across, so Ops chartered a plane.

Support services

Airlines make use of a vast range of service companies, from cleaners to caterers; refuellers to printers and designers. Most companies are independent, contracted to airlines to supply their services.

Ticketing

To buy and sell airline travel, ATOL (Air Travel Organizer's Licence) regulations state that the seller must be an airline, an airline ticketing agent, an ATOL holder or an agent of an ATOL holder.

To be able to work in this sector, you need to take a Fares and Ticketing Course. Contact IATA, or TTC (the Travel Training Company) for information on their TTC/Lufthansa Fares and Ticketing Course, approved by IATA: www.ttp@ttctraining

Case Study

Jennie worked for South African Airlines in reservations, who sent her on a ticketing course.

'I started my career with no formal training, leaving school at 16 with some GCSEs to work at Thomas Cook. They asked me what I wanted to do and I told them 'booking clerk'. But all the other school leavers wanted to do the same, and being the most junior I had to start at the bottom as a mail clerk. In a large organization like Cook's, there are many areas for promotion. I moved to being a debitor, then an itinerary clerk, then an individual inclusive itinerary clerk – checking a traveller's itinerary, making bookings for hotels, car hire, etc. I left Cook's to join the reservations team at Middle East Airlines, who trained on the spot. At that time, it was a manual system. Then I went on to South African Airways, where I was retrained on computer systems.'

When do airlines recruit?

Recruitment is almost continuous, with most airlines having large personnel departments or agencies to handle their interviewing. Look out for adverts in national newspapers or trade magazines.

Qualifications and training

You can find that the British education system lets you down. You may work incredibly hard to get good grades at school, but will they have any credibility with employers? And before you sign up for any course promising it 'fits you for a career in aviation' think – and think again.

John Clare, Education Editor of the *Daily Telegraph*, recently wrote of AS (Advanced Subsidiary) levels: 'Those who have suffered most are able pupils at good schools whose teachers failed to understand how dumbed down the exam has been... it is now clear that all the government-backed Qualifications and Curriculum Authority (QCA) had envisaged was an extension of GCSE, embroidered with some academically vacuous "key skills".' He then quoted a school governor writing about her daughter's class: 'She and her friends deserve an unreserved apology from the Department for Education and the QCA for the distress they have been caused.'

GNVQs have been another disaster. How often do you see adverts asking for these 'qualifications'? Recently one trade association rewrote their sector's GNVQ to reflect what their members wanted. When the unit was published they were horrified to discover their work had been discarded and students were being asked (again) to gather 'evidence' for paper-based 'projects' 'of no use to anyone'.

Tip!

Before you sign up for ANY course or qualification, ask employers and people working in the industry if the qualification will be of use to you. And *listen to them*, not to a college admissions official who only wants to get you signed up so the college can claim your tuition fee from the government.

The good news is that bureaucratic paperwork almost sank VQs, but a new Air Cabin Crew Vocational Qualification, developed with the industry, is now offered at colleges around Britain. The qualification includes:

◆ health and safety (including simulated evacuation from a smoke-filled cabin);
◆ first aid;
◆ operating emergency equipment;
◆ dealing with pax (passengers) during abnormal, dangerous

or emergency situations (training is very realistic in a simulator);

◆ preparing catering trolley and serving products;

◆ dealing with payments;

◆ dealing with pax complaints and incidents.

Colleges add in Fares and Ticketing and/or Level 2 NVQs in
Food Service and Hotel Reception, Foreign and Sign
Language, IT and Key Skills. Some colleges include hair and
beauty. For more information see www.eal.org.uk, telephone
(01923) 652400 or contact Pan Aviation Training Services.

Generally, an airline starts you off with an induction programme, whose length depends on the type of work you choose
to do. Most airlines have a well-defined career structure and are
particularly good at training. But realizing their training is very
intensive, many are keen to look at students who have taken
relevant preliminary training such as the new Air Cabin Crew
VQ, languages, a good marketing or business studies course, etc.

Case Study

BA's 'Putting People First' scheme.

One of the most ambitious training programmes was BA's 'Putting
People First'. Adapted from an SAS (Scandinavian Airlines Systems)
training programme, this literally saved the airline. Previously it had
become an uncaring giant. Frequent flyers instructed their travel agent:
'Book me on ANY flight but BA.' Luckily, the top brass saw something
drastic had to be done to save BA before the airline went bankrupt – and
seminars 'Putting People First' were rolled out.

Looking around these seminars, you found that there wasn't a single
colleague from your sector; engineers were mixed with telephonists,
cleaners were there too, office and administrative staff, one or two pilots
– in fact it was as though a computer had brought together people from
as many different departments as possible – which was the plan.
Barriers broke down, so staff were talking to each other about problems,
and actually suggesting they worked together to sort them out. Staff were
motivated to work together, which meant better customer service.

Tip!

Training is one of the busiest sections in any airline. It isn't only the preliminary training for pilots, engineers and cabin crew – but airlines are constantly training staff. Pilots have to do serious retraining every few months; cabin crew need to be kept up to date with safety procedures, and airlines constantly strive to improve customer care – which means more training.

Perks

If you want a change from routine in an operations job, most airlines ask for volunteers to look after 'unaccompanied minors' – or young children travelling on their own. Generally 'aunties' or 'uncles' accompany children in their spare time; usually each staff member is in charge of 10 kids. You fly to some wonderful places, and often strike up friendships with the kids. This activity comes to a peak at the beginning and end of school holidays, and each flight to destinations where parents are stationed is packed. Arthur Reed in his book *Airline* tells the lovely story of community singing (not unknown on these flights), which was so much fun that passengers in first class complained. They felt left out and wanted to join in.

One advantage of working for an airline is subsidized travel. However, aircraft often are fully booked and staff are the first to be off-loaded in favour of paying customers. A break in an exotic resort can turn into a weekend at the airport.

Under 18?

You can still prepare by taking courses that will be useful and look good on your CV:

◆ Air Cabin Crew VQ;

◆ First aid course (run by the Red Cross or St John Ambulance);
◆ four-day course in Health and Safety offered by many local government Environmental Health Departments.

It is also a good idea to do the following:

◆ Read a quality newspaper every day; you will be asked general knowledge questions at your interview.
◆ If you are taking a GNVQ, make sure it includes Travel Geography.
◆ Help out with a local charity looking after people.
◆ Apply to a local airline for work experience. This is difficult to find, but it is there. You have to be 16 or over, and for safety reasons most airlines won't allow work experiencers on board aircraft.

At Stansted KLM uk says it can only offer one-week place-ments due to the large number of requests. It has two types of placement. The first is in the head office, where duties include helping the departmental manager and team with administra-tion: filing, telephone work, data input and general work. The second is at the Stansted terminal and includes duties in the domestic and international departure satellites, alongside a customer agent, assisting with boarding outbound aircraft, checking passports/boarding passes, observing check-in and assisting with labelling hold baggage.

3 Working at airports

Everyone will agree that there is a magic to working at an airport, particularly at night when you have finished a long shift and know you have helped countless people with their travel problems.

Airports can be run by local authorities, be privately owned or be part of a large plc. In some cases, it is the airport operator who is the employer (for management, administration, baggage handling, maintenance, cleaning, information, apron control, medical services and emergency services). Other employers may be private companies based at an airport and operating a franchise on behalf of the airport.

UK airports handled 180 million passengers in 2000, a rise of 7 per cent on 1999. Although events such as the foot-and-mouth outbreak, the Lockerbie plane crash and the World Trade Center terrorist attack can cause a dramatic decrease in passengers, people want to travel, so eventually figures climb again.

Recently there has been a boom in low-cost airlines. To keep fares down, they have to cut out all frills – which often means landing at 'secondary' or lesser-known airports where charges are lower. These airports are often some distance from the city – but if you live on that side of a city, you are only too happy to fly from near home! Business travellers who might have an appointment near the airport are happy to save money, and student travellers and others on low budgets often don't mind if they have to make a journey of two or three hours to get into a city, if it means saving several hundred pounds on an air fare. This means more work at regional airports.

Airport authorities

Running an airport is a very complicated and, let's face it, stressful occupation. To run a major airport such as Charles de Gaulle in Paris, Schiphol at Amsterdam, O'Hare (world's largest) in Chicago, etc, requires a bigger budget than many small countries!

To get this big, airport administration will have gone out to 'sell' facilities to airlines and tour operators. It is no use having a superb airport with every facility imaginable, if passengers don't want to fly there.

Here are some of the reasons for passengers choosing to fly to or from one airport rather than another:

◆ being near a major destination for business or pleasure;
◆ cheaper than a competing airport, but still within relatively easy reach of a prime destination;
◆ runways long enough for larger planes to land;
◆ having a large catchment area.

So airports have to 'sell' themselves to airlines. They might be able to offer better engineering facilities, larger hangars, faster check-ins, etc, but the main selling point will be location, location – and price for each landing and take-off. Airlines pay the price determined by a complicated equation every time an aircraft lands. Recently, EasyJet threatened to leave Luton Airport, as landing charges had been increased from just over £1 per passenger to nearer £5. The low figure had been an introductory rate to encourage the airline to base itself at the airport. Once established, Luton increased the charges.

Airports encourage tour operators to use their airport to fly clients off on holiday. Again, price comes in to the equation, and also tour operators will want to see how many people live in the catchment area. They analyse their client base to see how many clients live near the 'new' airport, as opposed to the airport from which they currently fly, before deciding to add flights from this airport.

Look at an airport on a map, and you see a huge area. Within this is a multitude of jobs:

- BAA (British Airports Authority) employs 13,076 at its airports.
- London Heathrow Airport has 80,000 working there.
- 'Smaller' airports, such as Birmingham, Teesside, Belfast, etc, employ over 80,000 passenger sales agents, immigration officers, air traffic control staff, police, etc.
- Customs and Excise has around 24,000 employees.
- Support people, such as advertising and PR staff, freight agents, chaplains, animal health workers, etc, are also employed.

The recent BBC TV series *Airport* gave a very positive view of working at an airport, and skilful editing brought out the personal qualities needed from staff.

Airport work will almost certainly involve shifts, and you may need your own transport to cope with early or late starts. You have to be a good team member, particularly at peak times. Airline delays can mean working late into the evening to clear a backlog. This plays havoc with social life, but does give a sense of job satisfaction.

You and your colleagues have to sort out the knock-on effect of problems elsewhere: an unexpected influx of asylum seekers; a strike by air traffic controllers in another country; a hi-jacked aircraft trying to land at your airport. These and thousands of other problems mean that no day is ever the same.

Airports are expanding, and 'old' airports upgrading, so more jobs are available. Up to now it has been business traffic that has called the shots at major airports. This section had the money to pay ticket prices that included higher landing fees, and demanded quick access into the centre of cities. Holidaymakers flew from cheaper airports, often away from expensive central locations. However, recently Heathrow Airport announced that its traffic is split almost 50/50 between business and leisure. Europeans are taking more and more short breaks, and although in the United States it is still the norm for the average person to get only two weeks' holiday a year, this is bound to increase.

Recently, Birmingham Airport announced new destinations including Dubai, Islamabad, Karachi, Lahore, Marseilles, Prague, Cologne, Dubrovnik and Luxor. So airlines or their ground handling company will be requiring staff who speak the appropriate languages. Keep an eye out for press announcements like 'Airline X is opening a new service to...' This generally means that extra ground staff will be required.

Jobs at the airport

Administration

Queuing for your flight, you may see doors marked 'No Entry'. These lead to the administration offices where people are working to ensure your aircraft arrives and leaves on time, with the right amount of catering on board, cleaned, refuelled and with an accurate weather forecast to help the captain avoid a bumpy flight. Also needed are porters, cleaners, passenger service agents, and information, retail and catering staff.

Architect

There is hardly an airport that hasn't announced plans for expansion. Schiphol in the Netherlands has been snapping at Heathrow's heels for years, and recently announced forward planning that envisages an airport being built out in the North Sea, before Schiphol runs out of space.

Architects are developing more and more exciting airport plans in this international marketplace, especially in Eastern European countries, where German, Italian and Turkish companies are busy building. At last, passengers are genuinely being considered – if you go on holiday to Antalya Airport, look around you at the fantastic use of space with its calming effect.

Chaplain

Most international airports have an interdenominational chapel, with a chaplain in charge. As well as comforting people, chaplains are in demand for weddings of airport staff, and christening their children.

Engineering department

Some airlines will have a contract for aircraft maintenance rather than employ their own staff. There will almost certainly be a team of air traffic engineers, who are specialists in electronics, maintaining Air Traffic radar and aircraft landing systems. There will also be ground lighting technicians, whose job it is to see that the vitally important landing lights are working, plus general lighting.

Finance department

This is a very important section of airport administration, especially as it collects landing fees from airlines. The department is usually large enough to include support staff such as receptionists, secretarial and administration.

Fire Service

Every airport has to have a Fire Service, trained to carry out fire and rescue duties in emergencies. It also undertakes maintenance, inspections and testing of fire-fighting/protection systems/equipment. It is responsible for Fire Prevention Training, providing first aid treatment, giving disabled passenger assistance, snow clearance and de-icing. It also has to keep the airfield free of the birds that can cause a crash.

Information assistant

Most airports have a uniformed staffed information desk, answering queries from the public, airport staff, etc. Languages are definitely required for this job, including sign language. Staff also provide information working on a telephone switchboard. They update the flight information display system with arrivals and departures, make public address announcements, and so need a good speaking voice.

If you don't speak the customer's language, and they don't speak English, you must be able to work out what their language is so you can find an interpreter. If you speak the appropriate language you may be called on to interpret for the police, immigration or customs services. You will need to know customs procedures, as many questions will be about contacting friends or relatives who haven't yet passed through the customs hall – and may be held for questioning. You need a 'squirrel' mind that hoards masses of information, and the ability to recall where you can find the answer to thousands of questions – all different. You also need to be able to read timetables and maps, and know what to do with items handed in as lost property. An important duty is keeping up to date with emergency procedures, as it will be your job to assist with the evacuation of your terminal in the event of an incident.

Salary

Current salary £19,500 pa at Heathrow, plus uniform and subsidized canteen.

Case Study

Yolanda Perez-Lewis *works as an information assistant at Heathrow Airport.*

'Being part of the information desk team is great fun. A good sense of humour is a must and helps when dealing with some of our "interesting" members of the public – mind-reading abilities are useful too. One passenger spoke limited English, and wanted to know how she could save her marriage. We finally worked out it was her Air Miles that she wanted to save.'

> ## Tip!
>
> There are other information and sales desks at airports: hotel booking agencies, tourist information, car hire, mobile phone hire, bureaux de change, etc.

Maintenance

This department ensures the airport runs efficiently, and looks welcoming. It is responsible for maintaining the airport's vehicles, running repairs on airport buildings, and ensuring gardens and 'green' areas are looked after. Jobs in this section include mechanics, workshop fitters, welders, paint sprayers, plumbers, carpenters, decorators, etc.

Manager, service delivery

MSDs are directly responsible for managing the terminal operation on a shift-by-shift basis, working closely with airlines and control authorities. They need excellent leadership and team-working skills, sound judgement in order to deal with diverse situations, and an all-round knowledge and understanding of terminal operations. They also have to ensure that airlines obtain good service from the airport, the airport gets a good revenue, and, all the while, that passengers and staff are safeguarded by constant risk assessments and safety inspections.

Medical staff

Every airport has a fully staffed medical centre.

Operations

As well as administration, safety and the environment come under this department. There will be several health and safety committees, who supervise or monitor everything from noise and transport to encouraging good relations with the local community.

Personnel (sometimes known as human resources or HR).

It is this department's job to fill vacancies for administration staff, and airport support staff generally. It should be the department you contact when phoning for a job.

Sales and marketing department

They require staff to organize promotional events for the airport, liase with media regarding announcements, develop new routes and destinations, direct marketing campaigns and possibly liase with travel agencies in the region to promote the airport to their clients.

Security

Security staff prevent unlawful interference with civil aviation, and protect passengers, crew, other staff, aircraft, airfield installations and airport properties.

Today airports need a large security section, generally headed by a security manager. Under the manager are supervisors, training officers and security officers. Aviation security is a specialist vocation and heavily regulated by the Department for Transport (DTLR). Once accepted, staff undergo training on-site, with refresher courses when required. The job involves:

- physically searching passengers;
- watching and X-raying baggage;
- operating X-ray, archway and hand-held metal detectors;
- checking CCTV and alarm systems;
- searching airport terminals and surrounding areas;
- checking passes.

Technical services/IT department

They are in charge of the airport's technical, information technology and communication systems.

Terminal manager or airport duty manager

Remember the terminal manager in the recent BBC TV series *Airport*, always on the go? Her job was never boring as she prepared to face new challenges every day.

A terminal manager (TM) is in charge of a terminal at an airport with several terminals, eg Charles de Gaulle, Heathrow, etc. An airport duty manager (ADM) might be in daily charge of a small regional airport, or a mega-sized airport such as Frankfurt or Miami.

TMs and ADMs work shifts during an airport's operational hours. Their patch extends across airport buildings and runways, to the approach roads. If there is a major incident: fire, power failure, terrorist alert, etc, it is their job to implement emergency procedures.

Case Study

Stephen Golden, one of BAA's ADMs at Heathrow.

'No two shifts are the same and each day brings its challenges and rewards.' Stephen can never be sure what the next challenge will be: in the line-up to meet a head of state jetting in, or managing the problems caused by an aircraft with a burst tyre blocking a runway.

ADMs need to be able to assess situations quickly, use sound judgement to manage major incidents, and to 'have a sense of humour'. ADMs represent the airport at meetings with airlines that use their airport, and like a general manager of a large company, they have to satisfy customers and franchisees, by ensuring that their airport not only has the highest standards of safety, cleanliness and punctuality, but also is cost efficient.

Veterinary staff

The Animal Reception Centre at Heathrow looks after animals that fly in to Britain: exotic species on their way to zoos, pets brought into Britain either under the Pet Travel Scheme or on their way to quarantine kennels if they come from a country outside the scheme, and animals in transit from one country to another.

It is run by the Corporation of London, and the job is so enjoyable that staff tend to stay for years – so there are seldom any vacancies. However, now the procedure is simplified for anyone bringing a pet in to Britain, the Centre may need more staff to handle the dogs and cats that will fly here. Believe it or not, under the current regulations, a pet flies out of Britain as excess baggage – on the return it comes in as cargo (which is usually more expensive).

Off-airport jobs

Advertising and PR jobs are often handled by outside agencies, even in the largest airports. Doyens of this work are Anne Kavanagh PR, which handles the consumer side of BAA, and Geoff Saltmarsh Partnership, which handles much of the work for Schiphol Airport in the Netherlands.

Airport offices cost too much to rent, so freight and parcels, packages and cargo are also generally supervised and organized off-airport. However, this type of traffic is very profitable and therefore important to airports, although airports don't handle as much tonnage as a port (major European airports such as Heathrow, Frankfurt, Amsterdam, Paris, etc, handle between 1 and 2 million tons each a year). Goods that come in by air are generally high value (diamonds, contracts and other papers) or perishable goods such as fruit and vegetables.

Case Study

The promotion of Luton Airport.

Luton Airport had a new terminal and decided to run promotions to encourage more tour operators to feature departures from their airport.

First they had to encourage operators to visit and see what was on offer. So they hired a promotions company, which invited a selected list of operators for a champagne breakfast on board a coach from London to Luton. No precious time was to be wasted, but the operators could get to know the airport personnel on their way to the airport.

Breakfast was best champagne, excellent croissants, fresh fruit and anything else the company thought would give an up-market image. As the coach arrived, guests were surprised to find it sweeping past the terminal and onto the runway. Split second timing ensured that the runway was free as the coach sped down the middle. Suddenly fire tenders swept alongside, sirens blaring, and escorted the guests into their meeting – demonstrating that Luton had some very impressive fire-fighting equipment. This had meant a great deal of planning with air traffic control – but the airport wanted to make the point that their equipment was the latest and best available.

Today, Luton features in many tour operators' holiday programmes.

Other work

Regulatory bodies and associations need staff, such as the CAA (Civil Aviation Authority). Safeguarding customers' money when they buy an airline ticket is one of its duties. It is the CAA that grants ATOL licences, and this licence protects payment. Anyone unsure about an airline can phone the CAA on 020 7453 6430 to ask if the agent has an ATOL licence.

Qualifications and training

For most jobs you need GCSEs (or equivalent) in English and Maths. The BAA recruits graduates for training in computing, finance and management services. The CAA sometimes recruits people with previous experience in airport operation for managerial positions. If your aim is to become an airport manager, consider a Diploma in Business Studies, to include transport options.

Degree courses in transport administration, management and planning are offered by a number of universities. Contact the Institute of Logistics and Transport for further information. (Institute of Logistics and Transport, Earlstrees Court, Earlstrees Road, Corby NN17 4AX; Tel: 01536 740100).

For most operations jobs you will need a good education and to be able to drive a vehicle with a manual gearbox. You must have experience of dealing with the general public. Previous security work with the Armed Forces, Police, Prison Service, or as a store detective, etc, would be extremely useful.

Working conditions

You will be expected to work shifts for the majority of jobs. This means being available for work 365 days a year. Depending on whether the airport is open 16/17 hours (Heathrow) or 24 hours a day (most airports used by holidaymakers), you will work either 8-hour shifts such as 0600–1400; 1400–2200 or 2200–0600, or 0500–1330 and 1330–2200. You will almost certainly need transport to cope with early starts/late finishes.

Career progression

Ground staff at airports with efficient management skills and qualifications can progress to Airport Manager. They usually have responsibility for specific areas such as security, safety, and operations at the airport.

Don't just think of working at Heathrow or Gatwick – although Heathrow (LHR) is the busiest and Gatwick (LGW) the fourth busiest in passenger throughput in the world. Instead, look at local or regional airports, even airports around the world.

----------------------------------- **Case Study** -----------------------------------

Norwich Airport *is a busy regional airport for business and leisure pax (passengers).*

Its catchment area is Norfolk, Suffolk and Cambridgeshire. Principal scheduled services fly to Scotland, Paris and Amsterdam. Charters fly to Mediterranean resorts and other holiday destinations. There are also day flights to European cities.

Opened in 1933 for light aircraft, it was used by the RAF during World War II. Afterwards it was bought by Norfolk County Council, which developed it to take larger aircraft. In 1999, the airport became Norwich International Airport, and is fairly unusual in that it employs most of its staff, such as handling agents, information and customer services, security, air traffic control, technical services, retail staff, fire service, maintenance, administration including marketing, accounts and personnel.

Franchise companies such as car hire, foreign exchange, Customs and Excise, immigration, flying schools, helicopter operations, catering and cleaning, all employ their own staff directly. Currently planes are 'positioned' – flying in with their crew to pick up passengers at Norwich from another airport. The main airlines are KLM uk, Suckling Airways and Eastern Airways for scheduled flights, and Britannia, Caledonian, Air Europe, etc, for charter flights. There is also an expanding day tour market to Iceland, Florence, Barcelona, Oslo, Venice, etc.

Norwich recruits nationally for air traffic controllers, technical/electronic engineers and qualified fire fighters. But customer services, baggage handling and security staff are recruited locally.

4 Cabin crew

Cabin crew are on an aircraft for SAFETY reasons. Legally they are on board in the highly unlikely event of there being an accident, to usher passengers to safety. It is their duty to give safety announcements before a flight, or ensure that these announcements are given out on a video. They also ensure the safety of passengers by checking seat belts are fastened, and that hand luggage is secure. During the flight they may serve food and drink and sell duty-free goods. See the www.aviation-training.org Web site for more on cabin safety.

British Airways (BA), say cabin crew, 'are responsible for delivering the service experienced by customers in our aircraft cabins. Probably no other area within British Airways, or any other airline, has been subject to greater stereotyping and misperception. Some of this is down to the popularity of air travel. People see our cabin crew in action, often when they are relaxed or on holiday, and form an immediate impression of what they think the job involves. In fact, the customer sees only a fraction of what goes on in order to make each flight a success. What's more, whilst the cabin crew on board our aircraft form the largest part of cabin services, there are many other specialists supporting and driving this vital function.'

So cabin crew are the visible tip of an iceberg, with support services forming the hidden eight-ninths.

The first airline to employ cabin crew on a regular basis was probably the American airline Pan Am. Since then, it has become one of the most popular 'wish' jobs.

Employers

There are two main types of airlines: scheduled and charter. Both require crews Some private planes also employ their own cabin crew. Scheduled airlines such as BA, British Midland, Buzz, Go, United Airlines, KLM, SAS, Singapore Airlines, Emirates, etc operate a variety of routes and publish their timetables in a schedule.

Charter carriers such as Air 2000, Monarch, Britannia, etc can belong to a tour operator, or hire their aircraft to an operator. Tour operators may take up all the aircraft's seats for their package holidays, or split the seat allocation between package holiday passengers and 'seat only' sales. Or an airline may split the seats in aircraft between two or more operators.

Many Gulf airlines employ European staff. Emirates, who consistently win awards from travellers and magazines, employ the best from around the world. They have 48 different nationalities among their flight crew.

Qualifications

Most airlines have specific requirements for people applying for jobs as cabin crew:

- the right to live and work in the country where you will be based;
- minimum age generally 20+;
- excellent health and good eyesight but contact lenses usually accepted;
- height generally from 5 ft 2 in to 6 ft 2 in (1.57m–1.87m) with weight in proportion;
- MUST be able to swim – this is a legal requirement in case a plane has to ditch over water;

- good standard of general education;
- clear speech and good spoken English;
- customer service experience;
- passport that can be validated for travel to all countries covered by an airline's routes;
- car driver and owner or have means of 24-hour transport to base.

Languages: don't even think of applying to a European airline unless you speak English plus the airline's language fluently. On Crossair they expect you to speak English, French, German, Italian – just for starters. Once BA was considered a joke, with its 'if you don't speak English we can't be bothered to communicate' attitude. In the 'old' days I frequently found myself translating for bewildered passengers who found the BA crew didn't speak their language. BA's Putting People First campaign changed that; on a recent flight between Heathrow and Miami an announcement in excellent German came over the speakers. Many Germans find it cheaper to fly to London and then transfer to a Miami flight, so on this particular route BA make sure some of the crew speak German. Now it is difficult to find a job with BA unless you speak another language. If you can produce sign language, that is extremely useful.

What makes a good crew stand out? 'Personal appearance and manners with patience are vital', says Daniel Clarke of BA. 'Health is also vital and plenty of sleep.'

NB. Staff on some of the low-cost, no-frills airlines give safety announcements, sell refreshments, and then on arrival, when the passengers have left the plane, they clean the aircraft.

How to apply

There is tremendous competition for jobs, so you need to take care over your application. Before you even start the long process, make sure you have the legal right to work for an airline. You must either be a national of the airline's country, or have the legal right to work in the airline's country or be able to obtain this.

1. Contact the airline for an application form. If you are on the Web, most airlines today put these up on their Web site, or give you details of how to apply on their site.
2. Others want you to phone for an application form – see Chapter 13 for telephone numbers of some of the more popular airlines.
3. Or you might have a preliminary interview by phone.

Whatever airlines ask for, make sure you provide exactly the information they require. For example, if asked for a full-length photo, DON'T send in head and shoulders only.

Fill in the application form very, very carefully, and keep a copy. If you make it through to the face-to-face interview, you will be quizzed on what you put on your form.

The interview

Before you go for your interview, read Chapter 11, and remember, if you are turned down after the interview, always apply again. Many successful applicants were turned down on their first interview.

Training

This is taken extremely seriously; once qualified, in the event of an accident it is you and your colleagues that day who will be responsible for the lives of those flying in 'your' aircraft. Normally training takes about four to six weeks, and covers:

◆ health and safety procedures including administration of first aid and oxygen, evacuation procedures, etc;
◆ customer care;
◆ pre-flight checks of catering and cabin supplies;

- in-flight service including food, drink and refreshments;
- on-board sales and accepting payments in various currencies and credit cards;
- post-flight checks of on-board sales;
- body language;
- cultural awareness;
- care of special needs and disabled passengers;
- security duties.

You will be given talks about dealing with problems, from drunks to air rage. Anti-terrorism procedures bring stark reality into the classroom, but you have fun learning about grooming and looking after yourself.

You will be told about different passengers and how to look after them, which hand to use when serving food, tips for dealing with squalling babies, etc.

Don't even think about meeting friends or having a private life during training. You will be in classrooms from early in the morning until late at night, and then you have to revise into the small hours.

Preliminary training

What can you do to further your chances of being accepted by an airline? Try to find some suitable work experience – especially with a charity looking after people.

Take the Air Cabin Crew Vocational Qualification course. Over 400 ex-trainees have been accepted by Air 2000, bmi, GO, Palmair European, Britannia, BA, Air France, Gulf Airlines, JMC, Ryan Air, JAL, etc. Linda Holt, cabin crew manager recruitment and training, of KLM uk says 'We are very supportive of the cabin crew VQ qualification. Several of our current cabin crew have achieved this qualification before joining the airline and it has been very beneficial to them. The course content is very relevant, and we support several colleges (Norwich City, Leeds, Lowestoft, Bournemouth).'

Pat Egan of Pan Aviation Training Services helped set up this qualification, and says 'We have had 93 per cent achievement in our Air Cabin Crew VQ to date' with colleges from Carlisle to Portsmouth currently offering this VQ.

Case Study

Tessa *started as a stewardess with Britannia Airways, then moved to the administration unit as ground staff.*

'My stewardess job was my first since school; I got the job by applying to an ad in the paper. They required English GCSE and two others. After sending in an application with photo, I was called with several others for an interview. They talked to us individually about our family and social life and then gave us a simple maths test. After that, they split us into small groups to work on an imaginary plan of campaign involving travel arrangements. If you pass all that and your weight and measurements are all right, you also have to take a medical before you are taken on as a trainee.'

In Tessa's case, the course was a six-week one that included first aid (with an exam) and training for emergencies and cabin sales before she 'got her wings'.

Working environment

Working for an airline sounds glamorous – in reality it is very hard work. Experienced staff get the long-distance flights with stopovers. New staff are allocated domestic routes (flights within a country) or package tour destinations. These can mean being on your feet for 14–18 hours, doing two or three back-to-back flights.

Although airlines often emphasize they want 'team players' for cabin crew, on major airlines you don't meet the rest of your team until you gather an hour before the flight at the pre-flight briefing. It would be far too difficult to roster staff as a team, rather than individuals.

Normally, cabin crew have eight days off a month. Usually you receive your duty roster (timetable) a month in advance, but some airlines supply weekly or even daily rosters. In your roster, you may be allocated 'stand by' duties: waiting at home or at the airport to cover in case a colleague is unable to fly.

Tip!

Many airlines send out crew rosters by e-mail. If you don't have e-mail facilities, now is probably the time to think about investing in a computer. However, before you buy a 'cheap' one abroad, make sure that you will be able to get technical support at home. Jonathan from IBM says make sure your modem can be upgraded to V.92 standard, and your Internet service provider can support this. Thinkpads can do this and are easily portable. If you have an older machine – don't surf when waiting for a call – you don't want to miss the chance of a sudden overnight to an exotic destination because your rostering team can't get through! Telephone 0800 169 1458.

If your roster comes by phone, you need an answering machine. Make sure it is one that can take a long message (most cut out after 30 seconds). The BT Response 310 can take up to 13 minutes of message and has remote access. Telephone 0800 800 150.

Although you are paid a meal allowance when away, you have other expenses. Some US and other airlines make staff pay for their uniform. You will find you will be spending an enormous amount of money looking after your skin (men as well as women!) and even things like tights and socks can be more expensive.

DVT

Flying long distances can cause problems such as jet lag and tiredness. Recently DVT (deep vein thrombosis) has been highlighted as a problem for flyers, but cabin crew may not suffer this for two reasons: they are active the whole time, and many female staff wear support hose (tights worn by pregnant women). Wolford make 'Long Distance' tights that may help prevent DVT, and are more glamorous than support tights. For men, Scholl make support stockings.

Commission

Once you start flying, you make extra on commission from on-board sales, which are crucial to some airline operations. 'Why do you think charter crews flog everything so hard?' sniffed a purser. When tour operators' holiday sales are down, sometimes the only profit they make from clients is from on-board sales.

Airlines spend fortunes on glossy in-flight magazines to sell products. A charter airline like Airtours will have a winter and a summer magazine; the winter one aimed at higher-spending clientele; summer at families. So the airline, the tour operator and the crew are all concerned with on-board sales.

Tip!

One purser with record sales says 'Always wear an aftershave or perfume that is sold on board. Provided you like it, it is so much easier to sell!'

Case Study

Promoting La Prairie.

So training given by companies that supply products for on-board sales is very important. You might wonder why crew are often seen in front of the silver and blue La Prairie displays in duty-free displays, until you learn that this Swiss company takes training very seriously, and commission on its products is worth having. Also, constant flying causes havoc with cabin crew's skin (men and women), so cabin crew themselves are good customers. Twelve per cent of La Prairie's sales are to men, and having studied the product the crew know that the creams are expensive because the ingredients make them effective.

When La Prairie decided to launch its Caviar Collection in Swissair's First Class cabin, it found that clients were eating the products rather than using them on their skin. Perhaps this was because they contain extract of caviar – Joan Collins swears that eating caviar keeps her looking young! So the company organized product training for cabin crew and sales soared – to crew as well as passengers. Caviar contains zinc and iodine, which help repair skin and counteract the effects of stress and jet lag.

Although using a top-quality product gives anyone a feeling of luxury, there is a serious side to skincare. A product such as cellular moisturizer not only prevents skin drying out in cabin air (and eventually cracking) but it also protects against sunburn. Even on the dullest day cabin crew are advised to use a moisturizer with a minimum SPF 15 factor against sun and pollution. For working in hot sunny climates, or at high altitudes, the higher the SPF the better – there is a Soleil Suisse face cream and a body cream that are both SPF 50. And if you wonder how air hostesses manage to keep make-up immaculate for 12 hours, Heather, my favourite stewardess, says she uses Skin Caviar Firming Complex on top of her moisturizer. She doesn't need to renew make-up, even after 12-hour stretches. And I call Retexturizing Booster my 'miracle worker', using it when I have had too many long-haul flights.

On their course Heather says they all gave a gasp when at the end of a fascinating lecture, the consultant showed them a jar of Skin Caviar Luxe Cream, and said it cost £200. Everyone said that they would never, ever pay that amount – but some people must as La Prairie says it constantly sells out of stock!

> ## *Tip!*
>
> 'I like selling – I know the products and always show them and make an effort, especially in first class – one passenger can easily spend £1,000 or more at a time.'

Every year the major suppliers put on an exhibition purely for BA cabin crew in its Compass centre. During the exhibition suppliers show off new products, and crew vote on which ones they think should be stocked on board as potential top sellers. Things like alarm clocks are always popular, and often win this section.

Looking after yourself

There is one aid that costs next to nothing – water. Crew are advised to drink at least 2 litres a day to counteract the effects of air in cabins. It takes fuel to provide fresh air changes in the cabin; fuel costs money, so if an airline can get away with fewer air changes per hour, it will.

Certain products go the rounds of staff as their manufacturers have made extensive studies into 'air travel stress' and what it does to skin. Rather than spend money on packaging, these companies employ huge teams of chemists and researchers, and really bother about problems encountered by cabin crew. Some names to look out for are Décleor, Guerlain, Prescriptives, Helena Rubinstein, and of course Clarins and La Prairie.

Sore lips are a big problem, and you will need those expensive 'lip treatments' rather than cream sticks. All the above companies make colourless treatment 'lipsticks'. To counteract dryness you see crew constantly 'spritzing' their faces with Liz Earle's Instant Boost Skin Tonic or Décleor Arome Floral. They also use Décleor Systeme Corps to counteract body skin dryness. Beware of the sun: the wonderful tan on your hostess's face is probably Guerlain's Terracotta foundation and powder. And Clarins are responsible for those super-tanned bodies with their Exfoliator and Self-Tan.

Want to see if a product works for you? Try the tester's test: ask for a sample and use it on one side of your face for two weeks. Use your usual cream on the other. This is the only test that really works – because no two skins are the same.

Tip!

For aching feet and legs try the models' tip: Clarins Lait Jambes Lourdes. There are many cheaper copies – but none work as well. And it smells good!

Is this the job for you?

Can you physically stand being on your feet for up to 18 hours a day? Rise above the nauseous smell of sick? Keep cool, calm and professional when faced with football louts, angry business people or screaming babies? Yes? Then you are on the way towards making a good crew member.

Case Study

A day in the life of a crew member.

'Your day (or night) starts in the airline offices with a briefing on the flight, any special passengers flying: VIPs, disabled, children, etc. You look around the crew room to see if you recognize any faces, then listen to find out where you will be stationed – at the back looking after economy passengers, in the middle in business class, or up front if the airline has a first class.

Once on board you have a quick look around 'your' area, before you start up the ovens if serving hot food. These ovens are extremely temperamental. Herman Wolke, when Head of Lufthansa SkyChefs, one of largest catering companies in the world, said his biggest problem was to discover an oven that could heat up bread rolls properly on an aircraft.

Looking around, you check that everything for which you are responsible is (you hope) on board: a 747 will have some 36,000 items to be loaded. You then stock up the trolleys; another temperamental piece of equipment – try steering these down a narrow aisle without stubbing your toes.

As passengers arrive, you help them find their seats and ensure seat belts are fastened. Then you go into the safety routine. Passengers tend to ignore these, but will be the first to complain if there is a crash and they don't know what to do.

In economy you are working constantly, serving drinks, food and then the important 'duty free'. If it's a short flight you only have an hour in which to do all this – on longer flights you sometimes have a moment to draw breath! And change your shoes, and perhaps put on a fresh pair of support socks or tights. You can fool your feet some of the time!

Up front crew sometimes have time to talk to passengers, especially those whom they recognize from previous flights. But most of the time you feel you are a cross between a waitress and a nanny. And guess who cleans up if someone is sick? And your working space is absolutely minimal, so you have to keep everything tidy and in its place. My mother peeked into our galley once, and then made comments about my own bedroom. But it is different when it is your work space. If you put something down in the wrong place, your colleagues can't find it.

Finally, the aircraft is coming in to land and you check everyone has fastened their seat belt and all packages, bags, etc, are stowed away. Once landed, you help passengers with bags, and smile and smile, hoping they had a good flight. Then comes the paperwork: bar sales, duty free, etc. It is the chief stewardess or purser's job, but we have to make sure we have handed in the correct details, money, etc. People don't realize how much paperwork is involved in this job.

Then the ground crew come on board to empty the waste tanks, replenish water, carry out an engineering check, which also means repairing faults in the cabin, and clean and tidy the cabin before the next passengers arrive, unless you work for one of the 'low-cost' airlines, when you will have to clean around the cabin yourself. Then passengers start to board and the routine starts again – unless you are on a long-haul flight, when you leave the aircraft and go off for your debriefing.

It is tiring and extremely hard work – but most cabin crew will tell you it still beats the 9–5 job.'

Medical matters

The first flight attendants had to have nursing qualifications and these are still useful. Recently, Emirates Airlines was awarded full accreditation to the Royal College of Surgeons of Edinburgh for its medical training for cabin crew.

In 1998, Emirates became one of the first airlines to equip its aircraft with defibrillators. These have proved their worth in saving lives. Each aircraft is also linked to MedLink, an Emergency Telemedicine Centre based at a hospital in Phoenix, USA. When medical emergencies occur in-flight, crew can phone in to the MedLink emergency centre from anywhere in the world via satellite communications lines on every aircraft. Dr Beatton, Emirates' Head of Medical Services, says 'The proficiency of our cabin crew in dealing with in-flight emergencies means that we make very few calls to MedLink. As a result, when a call comes in from an Emirates aircraft they take it very seriously indeed.'

Emirates are also concerned about DVT, and became the first airline to offer the Airogym, a simple cushion device that exercises the leg muscles whilst sitting on an aircraft.

Swissair was the first European airline to equip all its fleet with automatic external defibrillators for use in a medical emergency, followed by its sister airline, Crossair. Now most major airlines carry this equipment, or are seriously considering installing it.

Getting started

Most European airlines pay a small salary whilst you are training. Some American airlines warn applicants that they will need around $2,000 for expenses during training, as they don't receive a salary until qualified.

European airlines usually provide uniforms, but American airlines may also expect you to pay for your own uniform via payroll deductions every month.

Career progression

As cabin crew, you work your way up from the back to the front. Generally junior staff will be put on to serve the economy- or tourist-class passengers; eventually you can work up to number 2 or 3, moving up to purser, supervisor or chief flight attendant. With a large airline, you become a senior purser of a fleet, working your way up to the newest aircraft.

Then you might go on to be a line trainer (training crew on the differences between different aircraft), then a base trainer (general training) and eventually to a senior position at base, recruiting, training and organizing cabin crew.

Some cabin crew go on to work on a company or private jet. This can have its downside, as you wait on a lonely airfield at 3 am for your rock star employer to come on board from their concert, reeking of sweat, in a foul temper because they are so tired. The plus is you don't work so many long hours, and often have time to get out and see destinations.

Salary

Some no-frills airlines pay equivalent of £8,500 pa for a six-month contract = around £165 a week. GO's salary is around

£13,000 pa. Emirates offers a three-year renewable contact, tax-free salary of around £178 per week plus flying allowance of £50 per week, shared accommodation with own bedroom at base, comprehensive medical cover and end-of-service benefits.

Case Study

Pro Sky *is a broker for air charters.*

Clients go to Pro Sky to hire a plane for a private journey. Last autumn, 200 mobile phone sales staff won a trip to Dubai as a reward for exceeding sales targets. Pro Sky booked the plane, and added touches to ensure guests felt pampered.

As the winners checked in, their company logo was flashing on the screen of the specially reserved desk. Extra staff meant no one had long to wait on the smart red carpet. Once in the departure lounge, there were snacks and drinks whilst they waited to board their own specially chartered Boeing 757.

Pro Sky had briefed the crew, and written a special welcome speech that the captain broadcast as soon as they were airborne. Cabin crew served a gourmet meal, afterwards handing chocolates around, wrapped in foil printed with the company logo. During the flight the captain made special announcements tailored to the clients, giving them information on the route.

Eleven minutes after arriving in Dubai, passengers were on their coaches and being given a short guided tour, whilst the luggage went straight to the hotel. By the time the guests arrived at their hotel their luggage was waiting in their hotel bedroom.

Case Study

Air Partner

When Concorde was grounded, brokers Air Partner were approached by up-market tour operators Abercrombie and Kent. Abercrombie had organized a 3-week round-the-world tour, using Concorde. No Concorde – how were they to fly?

The answer was to fit out a special 747. In just six weeks, the aircraft underwent a transformation. Four hundred plus seats were torn out, and

106 luxury leather chairs fitted in their place. Each chair had a 60 in pitch (distance between the back of the seat and the front edge). The nose section became a cocktail bar, and 14 attendants, one for every eight passengers, were hired to serve five-course gourmet meals.

Currently this is the largest passenger aircraft in the world available for charter, and it wasn't long before the orders rolled in. After the tour it flew to French Guyana, carrying VIPs to watch a satellite launch, and then special racks were fitted to cradle cases of wine – for a wine lovers' tour.

5 Customer/passenger service agents (CSAs/PSAs)

CSAs/PSAs provide a 'handling' or welcome service for passengers from arrival at the airport until they finally board their plane. In the United States, this job description also covers working as a ticket sales agent at an airport.

In the BBC's *Airport* the Aeroflot PSA needed to be a strong character to cope with Russian passengers who thought the plane would wait for them whilst they finished their shopping. Would you have remained good tempered, got your point across and managed to get 'your' plane off on time?

Employers

Employers fall into two groups. First, airlines that employ their own staff to check in their passengers. Second, ground handlers providing check-in services on behalf of airlines, probably because these airlines don't have enough flights to justify employing their own staff full-time.

The job

Duties include:

◆ check-in;
◆ seat allocation;

- ◆ baggage: weigh and tag;
- ◆ checking travel documents;
- ◆ accompanying passengers to and from the aircraft;
- ◆ dealing with lost or damaged property;
- ◆ assistance for disabled and special-needs passengers;
- ◆ looking after unaccompanied children;
- ◆ assistance in the case of delays.

The PSA's job is vital in getting passengers and baggage onto the aircraft on time. Aircraft are allocated a 'slot' or time to take off. Miss that, and with today's overcrowded skies, the aircraft might have to wait an hour or more for a new take-off slot. So the PSA has to check everyone in and get them to the departure gate on time.

Of course passengers, especially those arriving late, will stop to buy duty frees, thereby holding up the plane. It is the PSA's job to get them to the gate before the captain loses his or her slot. Surprisingly, even after checking in around 400 passengers for one flight, you have a rough idea of which passengers are on board, and a quick run through the departure lounge usually turns up the missing passenger – browsing around the shops and totally oblivious of the trouble they have caused. But if you can't find the absentee, their luggage has to be unloaded; when the passenger turns up... you keep your temper as you tell them why their luggage won't be on the aircraft.

Some PSAs work on the ticket desk, selling tickets, issuing pre-paid or pre-booked tickets, and re-issuing tickets for passengers whose flight details are amended at their request or through delays or cancellations. In emergencies, ticket-desk staff may also arrange taxis, accommodation, ticket refunds, and deal with finding 'mis-routed' baggage – never 'lost'!

Group check-ins are another facet of the job. It may be a football team flying off for a match, incentive conference winners being given VIP treatment, a tour group, etc. Many airlines have dedicated group check-in desks, or even arrange check-ins 'off' airport, for example in hotels. Much of the work is done beforehand, allocating seats, supplying boarding cards and arranging for the bulk transfer of luggage if security allows this.

Warning!

CSAs/PSAs bear the brunt of passengers' anger if their flight is delayed or cancelled. This is certain to escalate, due to increased congestion in the air. Be prepared for 'passenger rage' and try and inform people as soon as you know what is happening.

Although the job is almost the same if you are working directly for an airline, or for a ground handler, obviously you have more flexibility when something goes wrong if you are working directly for the airline.

Warning!

Until airlines universally agree to charge 'no show' passengers (passengers who book on a flight but don't bother to turn up), there will always be overbooking to compensate for the numbers of expected 'no shows'. If they all turn up, guess whose job it is to tell the passenger checking in 'Sorry – the flight is overbooked and there is no seat for you'? Got it in one.

Surprisingly, the vast majority of passengers accept overbooking fairly well – luckily there are few cases of PSAs being physically abused – but verbal abuse is par for the course. Well, how would you feel if told there isn't a seat? Some staff will retort 'I don't have to take abuse', and no, you don't. But, if you can't take it, you are not going to last long in the job. Your wages come out of passengers' ticket fees – polite and rude – so get in there, be as polite, cool, calm and helpful as possible, and you will be surprised how many passengers come up afterwards to apologize for their rudeness.

Tip!

There is often part-time work, especially during peak months.

Once you have done your apprenticeship on charters and over-booked flights, you may be offered a job checking in business, premium, first-class, etc, passengers. They aren't any politer than economy or tourist-class passengers, but at least they are fewer and there is more space. Most of them are seasoned travellers, so won't be wasting time but want to get on. Before the World Trade Center outrage, some airlines operated check-ins at the kerbside or away from busy areas. Once security measures have been addressed, business and first-class clients will expect their return.

Case Study

The PSA *in* Airline

Sadly, the recent *Airline* docusoap sometimes gave a bad impression of a PSA's work. Viewers were left with the impression that 'you get what you pay for' – true, but the airline business can suddenly become extremely competitive, and then customer loyalty can mean the difference between staying in business or closing. The old-fashioned words 'I'm sorry' don't commit you or your company, but can at least go some way towards turning a lemon into lemonade.

One *Airline* scene stood out. A flight arrived late, meaning a wheelchair passenger missed his connecting flight (by the same airline). Of course, conditions of carriage mean that often an airline is not obliged to do anything if this happens, especially on a low-cost airline (one reason why costs are kept low). However, most people would consider someone in a wheel-chair to be a special case. Eventually the airline did, but not until after time had elapsed and the poor passenger was left hanging around to find out his fate.

Ground handling companies

Most airports either operate a ground handling service or employ a company to do this on their behalf. Clients are airlines that don't have enough flights to justify 'handling' their own passengers, or for various reasons would rather employ another company to operate this on their behalf.

Meeters and greeters

These are sometimes called 'hunters', 'sweepers', or similar names. They float around purposefully in the mob waiting in front of check-in desks at peak times.

It is their job to make sure passengers are in the right queue, anyone who is delayed if possible gets pushed to the front, and when overbooking happens, to go along the queue of waiting passengers to find out if anyone will take money in return for flying the next day. As the departure time gets closer, so the 'inducement' is raised.

To help matters, some staff are now being issued with hand-held computers and they can check-in passengers in the queue.

Specialist staff

Most major airlines have specialist staff who deal with children, sick or elderly passengers, and VIPs. If you have had experience of looking after children or have a nursing qualification, these can be useful. American Airlines have Skycaare, which provides skilled medical companions for travellers who need limited medical attention and care during flights. These are registered nurses with advanced medical experience, training and qualifications, and passengers pay for the Skycaare attendants' flight, plus expenses.

Case Study

A day in the departure area.

To make all the different passenger service jobs come together, imagine you are leaning over the balcony, watching a busy departure area in an international airport. People scurry to and fro, but eventually you begin to see a pattern. At 9 am, almost all check-in desks are 'manned' by customer or passenger service agents, with long queues waiting. Word comes through that there is a baggage handlers' strike at Munich Airport – luckily the Lufthansa flights have mostly business travellers with carry-on luggage, so staff don't have to spend too much time explaining that the airline will be flying, but passengers with luggage that goes in the hold may experience delays.

Other airline staff are glad it isn't their day for delays, and get on with the morning rush hour. However, they also have problems with baggage. It is Fashion Week in Paris, and instead of the usual business traffic flying to Paris for the day, there are models and agents laden down with extra baggage. This not only means it has to be weighed but also excess baggage calculated and charged. Models are used to this, but some holidaymakers are not, and there are grumbles.

A ticket desk agent is dealing with an anxious passenger trying to buy a ticket for a flight leaving for Oslo at 0950. According to the computer the flight is full, but as departure time gets near it is obvious to experienced staff that there are going to be a lot of 'no shows', so she will be able to get on the flight. By this time it is getting late, so the agent runs through the departure lounge with her to get her on the plane on time.

Behind the scenes, the flight connect agent is worried about the Paris flight. He knows three models are flying in on a plane from Tokyo to connect with the next Paris flight – but their incoming flight has been delayed. Normally, with flights every hour or so to Paris, this wouldn't be a problem, but today all flights are fully booked with stand-by passengers waiting. It is his job to find the passengers and as they are travelling first class they should be first off the plane – on a Jumbo it can take half an hour for everyone to disembark. Then he will have to rush them and their baggage across to the Paris flight.

Down in BA's Skyflyers Lounge for young unaccompanied travellers, the Skyflyer Ground Escort suggests to one of her charges that it is time for him to leave his computer game and catch his flight. As it's term-time it's quiet in the lounge, but come the holidays and the place is packed. She takes the Skyflyer through immigration and security, being careful to let him lead the way – most are extremely sophisticated and don't like being patronized. At the gate she will hand him over to a crew member, with documentation confirming the name and contact details of the person meeting him. There are strict security checks to ensure that the right person meets a child, and Skyflyers aren't allowed to leave the airport until the corresponding ground staff have checked the person's credentials.

Qualifications

◆ age 18+;
◆ customer service experience;
◆ GCSEs or equivalent (grade C or above) in English and Maths;
◆ right to live and work in the country.

Also helpful are a full driving licence (you are expected to work shifts, which could start before public transport starts), and a second language. You should also be numerate and accurate when dealing with paperwork or working on a computer screen. Experience working with the general public, and particularly teamwork, is very helpful. You should also be:

◆ pleasant and outgoing;
◆ able to work fast and accurately to tight schedules;
◆ smart.

Training

For work on the ticket desk, a fares and ticketing course is useful, as is experience of working in a travel agency. The Air Cabin Crew Vocational Qualification includes passenger handling. So far, over 150 students have been accepted for PSA work by UK airlines. Contact Pan Aviation Training Services for your nearest college.

Case Study

Tho coriouc cido to boing a PSA.

There is a very serious side to this job. Because of terrorism, each passenger has to be asked if they have packed their bag themselves. Trained PSAs develop a sixth sense to evaluate the flippant answers.

And you have to know the law. According to the *Daily Telegraph*, a recent court case in the States left American Airlines and British West Indies Airline paying out £113,000 to the family of Caroline Neischer. Mrs Neischer had travelled from Los Angeles to Guyana in two legs, and had been allowed to carry on board her bag containing her asthma medication on the first leg to New York. At New York, a PSA forced her to check in her bag. Unfortunately, Mrs Neischer's luggage didn't arrive for two days, by which time she had been taken to hospital, where she died.

The family's lawyer said the decision was important to all travellers on international flights. 'For the first time under the Warsaw Convention, airlines have been held responsible for the callous removal and loss of baggage resulting in the death of a passenger.' Both airlines were held liable, even though it wasn't clear which airline's agent forced her to check in the bag, or why they did so. The actions of airline employees therefore constituted 'wilful misconduct' and Ned Good of the Consumer Attorneys of California said this 'should put all airlines on notice that medical equipment that is used in the active care of a passenger must be at the right place at the right time'.

Allied jobs

Aircraft movements

An aircraft doesn't have a reverse gear; once its doors are closed, drivers push the aircraft off the ramp, using a tug or tractor. You have to know what you are doing: moving 400 tons of plane with a 70-yard wingspan takes skill. The aircraft's movements team is also responsible for making sure aircraft are correctly positioned on their stands when they arrive, and before departure the aircraft's electrical and air-conditioning systems are plugged in to ground systems. Linked by intercom to the flight deck, the team are the captain's eyes and ears on the ground, making sure the area is cleared of any objects before the engines start up.

> ## *Tip!*
>
> If you don't like the cold, be aware that during winter, aircraft movements drivers will be working the de-icing equipment – and an airport can be one of the coldest places on an early winter morning.

Ramp services agent

These staff are responsible for the safe and timely loading–unloading of freight and luggage, to strict and rigid deadlines. The moment luggage is tagged by the PSA with a bar-coded label and sent off into the luggage system, it comes into the ramp services agent's territory. A computer scans the barcode and the luggage is automatically directed to be loaded onto a container. Once full, the container is directed towards the appropriate aircraft. Then Distribution loads it on the aircraft, making sure that they follow instructions from the aircraft despatcher, who will have already worked out the load sheet, deciding how much weight is to go into each hold. This job is vital to ensure that the aircraft is properly 'trimmed' to fly safely and at its optimum speed, consuming fuel efficiently.

Computerization has meant that if a passenger doesn't check in on time at the aircraft door, it is easier to unload their luggage. The ramp services agent will match the barcode with the passenger's boarding pass details on screen – and know immediately which container has their luggage. You juggle with problems whilst liaising with the captain in the case of delays that could make the aircraft lose its take-off slot.

Ramp services managers often represent their airline at meetings with airport administration and other airlines.

Getting started

It can be daunting to find a job as an agent. There are so many different employers, many of whom go under different names, or names that you might not associate with work. There are several ways in:

1. Contact the local jobcentre – those at Heathrow and Gatwick are often asked by employers to find staff.
2. Some airports offer their own ground handling. Phone the airport switchboard and ask to be put through to personnel or human resources.
3. If you want to work for an airline, go to your local airport and ask the information desk if they have a list of airlines that use their airport. This will usually list the scheduled carriers (airlines). Then ask if they have a list of charter airlines. Then walk around and keep your eyes open – watch the monitor screens for names of airlines, look out for tour operators' desks and see which airline their passengers fly by, and ask the staff checking in passengers how they found their job (when they aren't busy!).
4. Ask the information desk if you can have a copy of the airport newspaper. This will often list jobs, and you can read the news stories for names of airlines.
5. And of course, watch local newspapers for ads.

Is this the job for you?

You have to be able to work whenever the airport is open, which can be 24 hours a day. You have to handle angry passengers when there are delays, when a client thinks he or she should have been upgraded, and you have to say NO, when clients arrive with a large amount of baggage and you have to tell them they will have to pay for excess baggage, and when a travel agent has supplied a ticket for a child travelling solo, and the child turns out to be under the legal age limit for travelling on their own (when you are faced with angry parents and tearful children). And you have to keep your cool whilst ensuring that you continue checking in others in time to catch their flight.

But at the end of the day, working at an airport gives you a tremendous 'buzz', and many people stay there all their working life. You are meeting and helping people all day long, and the satisfaction you get from sorting out a problem, and enabling people to go on their flights, can give you a very, very warm feeling. If you have a good brain for administration but also like helping people and successfully sorting out problems, this could be the job for you.

And if at the end of all this, you are turned down when you go for your interview – don't worry. Every airline and airport needs agents – so look for another opening.

Trains

If you want work similar to that of cabin crew, but don't fancy flying, try Eurostar. Its staff serve food, and look after passengers on the trains. Only difference is you don't fly. Contact Momentum on 020 7902 3589.

Or try working for the ultra-smart Gatwick Express Train. Staff are needed for Victoria and Gatwick stations' information desks, inspectors who tell you where to go (in the nicest possible way) and trolley staff who bring refreshments around to your seat. Emma Swan says they look for people who are 'positively motivated, friendly and polite'. There are two different roles: platform customer service staff who provide information and help people to board the train at Gatwick or Victoria, and on-board staff who sell tickets, provide customer service and serve and sell refreshments from the trolleys. Phone human resources: 020 7973 5025.

The Heathrow Express also requires train staff: contact the BAA. PSA/check-in staff also work for major airlines at Paddington and Victoria stations.

6   Pilots

How to become a pilot

Once airlines trained their own pilots. Today they recruit from ex-Forces, other airlines or expect pilots to pay for their own training. So unless you are very, very lucky, the way in is either as ex-Forces, or paying for your own training.

BALPA (British Airline Pilots Association) says the way to become a pilot is either learn to fly with the Armed Services (become a trainee pilot if 17–24) or learn to fly privately and get your Private Pilot's Licence (PPL).

Once you have a PPL, you can fly for fun or work, but not commercially for 'hire and reward'. For this you need a CPL (Commercial Pilot's Licence), which you obtain by:

◆ moving from the Forces to an airline;
◆ or taking a training course at an approved school;
◆ or obtaining full or partial sponsorship from an airline.

Once you have your CPL, you can be a pilot of an aircraft for single-pilot operation.

To become a co-pilot in a commercial airliner you have to demonstrate a knowledge of theory at the Airline Transport Pilots Licence (ATPL) level.

To be a captain of an airliner you must actually hold an ATPL by passing an exam and flying 1,500 hours.

Cost

Marie Barlow, Course Administrator at Cabair College of Air Training, says that their general course costs £45,000 plus accommodation and exam fees. Occasionally, airlines will part sponsor a trainee – perhaps offering £10,000 or £20,000. Watch out for announcements in the Cabair ads in *Flight International* or *Pilot Magazine*. You will be competing against a lot of people for sponsorship, but don't despair. Marie says 'one chap tried 10 times before he made it. Now he is up there flying.'

Tip!

If you are going to university, or live near a university town, ask if they have an air squadron, as this could be a cheaper way to obtain training.

Career development loan (CDL)

Most would-be pilots bite the bullet and take out a loan to pay for training. The government offers CDLs up to £8,000 – you need savings or another loan to top this up. See details at end of this book. You can use a CDL to pay for CPL (not private flying) training abroad, but you must be a British citizen and guarantee to be based in the UK until the loan is paid off.

Tip!

Training is often cheaper in the US, even after playing for flight accommodation. One reason is because the weather is usually reliable, so you get in more flying time.

Case Study

Britannia Airlines' requirements.

Britannia, the world's largest charter airline, asks for a minimum of 200 hours logged flying time before it will even consider your application to start as a second officer. You have to hold a CPL/IR (Commercial Pilot's Licence/Instrument Rating). First officers have to have a minimum of 1,500 flying hours, of which 500 are on jets or 1,000 on Turbines, plus a UK ATPL. Other airlines ask for a minimum 1,500 hours flying experience.

Tip!

If you are going to pay for training, Zoe from the CAA says that before signing up for a flying course, it is worth checking out if you are fit enough to pass an airline's medical test. All prospective pilots (and current ones) have to pass very stringent medical tests, and it would be a shame to spend a lot of money on a course only to find out that you are not fit for flying. Ask your doctor about obtaining a Class 1 Medical Certificate, and have an eye check for visual acuity corrected to 20/20.

Sponsored training scheme

Some airlines have trainee schemes. One is the British Airways Sponsored Pilot Training Scheme. The airline knows that the huge cost of learning to fly has tended to put a career in commercial aviation beyond the reach of many young men and women, but now BA says 'Not only does our sponsored training scheme bring the career of a commercial airline pilot within the reach of everyone, regardless of background; those who successfully complete it have learnt to fly to the very highest standards.'

As you can imagine, there are thousands of applicants for any sponsored pilot training. However, if you are lucky enough to be accepted for training, most schemes last around 18 months.

During training, part of your costs will be met, including board and lodging. However, once qualified you are expected to repay these costs by deductions from your salary. To be eligible you must:

◆ be aged 18–26;
◆ possess a passport allowing unrestricted worldwide travel;
◆ be entitled to live and work in the EU without restrictions;
◆ have five GCSEs or equivalent at Grade C or above, including English Language, Mathematics and a Science subject;
◆ have two or more GCSE A Levels (or equivalent) in core academic subjects (except General Studies and some other subjects) at Grade C or above, or Hons Degree Class 2:2 or above or equivalent;
◆ have evidence of setting and achieving high standards;
◆ be between 5 ft 2 in and 6 ft 3 in with weight in proportion;
◆ be physically fit and able to satisfy JAA/UK CAA Licence Medical (Class 1) and BA medical requirements (stricter than CAA);
◆ have distance visual acuity of not less than 6/9 (20/30 or 0.7) in each eye separately, with or without use of correcting lenses;
◆ have fluent English;
◆ have a clear speaking voice;
◆ have confident communication skills.

You also have to show leadership qualities, have an analytical mind and able to understand technical problems. You must have good hand-to-eye coordination with good spatial aware-ness and the ability to read maps and three-dimensional displays. You must have a practical approach to life, excellent powers of observation and be able to pay close attention when working with figures. You must also be able to work as part of a team and get on with the public.

If you satisfy these criteria, and are chosen to go on the scheme, BA's training is a 70-week training programme.

The first 56 weeks are spent acquiring basic flying skills and working for a frozen Airline Transport Pilot's Licence (ATPL).

A frozen ATPL is when you have done the ATPL exams at the outset and just need the hours in flying experience to convert. Carolyn Evans from the BALPA says Stage 1 is the CPL; you cannot hold an ATPL until you have 1,500 hours. To upgrade when you have the required hours you then have to do the ATPL theory exams.

This is followed by the Jet Conversion Course to convert from piston to jets, and from single pilot to multi-crew ops. Once you finish this, you are then eligible for employment.

During the course you visit BA's operational and business areas, and take part in BA's charity functions providing support for the local community.

Lufthansa also offers pilot training for EU citizens. First, you must take a medical (at your own expense) at one of its approved centres in Germany. The next hurdle to pass is a two-and-a-half-day exam and assessment in Hamburg (at Lufthansa's expense). If you are then accepted on the course for training, Lufthansa part-sponsors this; you pay around 80,000 DM (£26,000, or approximately 40,000 euros) spread over 10 or 15 years.

Lufthansa offers an interesting degree in Aviation Systems Engineering and Management plus an ATPL. This is an eight-term course, with training in English and German. Studies take place at Bremen Polytechnic, with flying training in the US. For more information look on the Web site www.lufthansa.com or phone (49) 1803 547 4568.

Salary

Pilots working for major airlines earn between £50,000 and £120,000 a year. Recent articles in the *Telegraph* and *Daily Mail* quoted Michael O'Leary, boss of Ryanair, saying he is to boost the pay of his 220 pilots to over £80,000 a year – and give share options!

Career progression

You progress from second officer, first officer then captain. Once you have had experience in this senior post, you could become a line training captain, training others in the flight simulator – a machine that accurately duplicates everything that a genuine aircraft does, or can do, but is cheaper to run.

Or you could become involved in flight operations management, or develop training programmes for other staff.

Case Study

Mike Evans, pilot.

Yes, there are frustrations – even for captains! Mike Evans says that currently their worst problems are delays, which are escalating, especially across Europe. 'We are only allowed to fly 900 hours a year, and a lot of this time is spent waiting around as ATC has not been able to give us the slot we want.

Then delays on the ground add to problems. The other day I was so angry when my plane was held up at Rome that I went on the public address system to apologize to passengers – telling them the delay was due to the fact that the airport still hadn't enough baggage handlers.

My roster always seems to take in all the important events in the kid's lives. Every other captain seems to have kids of the same age! So unless I want to be across the other side of the world, I have to think six months ahead to put in for time off for school sports days every summer.

But there is something magical about flying over the great mountain ranges of the world. I always think of Hannibal climbing slowly up across the Alps, and wonder how the elephants coped. Then every time the Rockies come into view I am awestruck to think that to cross this massive mountain range that passes beneath my plane in a few minutes, took the early settlers weeks, if not months.'

Helicopter pilots

The British Helicopter Advisory Board has a Web site (www.bhab.demon.co.uk) on which it has a training section: 'I want to be a helicopter pilot'.

Ballooning

More and more companies are offering commercial balloon flights, for which they need qualified pilots. The best way to find out more is when you see a balloon in the sky, follow it to the landing (don't get in the way when they are landing) and ask questions – once the equipment is safely stowed.

Balloon flight companies may need staff to help inflate the balloon, follow the flight path on the ground, tether the balloon when it lands and stow it away.

7 Engineers

The work

Aircraft engineers

The public sees the captain as in charge of the aircraft. The captain knows the aircraft he flies is only as good as the maintenance carried out by the engineers, and major airlines will have around 10,000 engineers working on their aircraft.

Pilots need to have confidence that engines will fly their plane and not break down: in the early days this was a major cause of accidents.

Engineers need in-depth knowledge to service the very complicated machinery in today's aircraft and keep them flying. Arthur Reed in his book on BA quotes a Concorde captain: 'If you did not have faith in the engineers, you would be sitting on the edge of your seat the whole time. But we know that the aircraft are always presented to us for service in a first class condition, and that underlying faith in the whole maintenance procedure is shared by all our flight crews.'

Working in an airline's engineering department involves long and meticulous training. In most cases, airlines offer four-year maintenance engineering apprenticeships. Apply to the appropriate airline, but make sure you live near their maintenance base – some international airlines may work out of an international airport but will carry out maintenance at a smaller airport where costs are lower.

The CAA (Civil Aviation Authority), and its equivalents abroad, set out very exact schedules of maintenance for every type of aircraft: so many maintenance checks and replacements after so many hours' flying. Each aircraft has a logbook with detailed information about every check carried out, and the engineer in charge signs off each job. Every time an aircraft goes out of the engineering base, the technicians who have lovingly serviced this machine know that if anything happens because of a fault overlooked, it will be traced back to them. They have to be good.

The only time the engineering department gets to service an aircraft is in the 'down' time – when it's not flying. Short checks can take place in between flights – longer checks have to be carried out overnight. Sometimes an aircraft has to be taken out of service, which is not popular with the financial department or operations.

Engineering departments use incredibly sophisticated diagnostic equipment. There will be X-ray machines (encased in concrete and lead-lined doors), scanners and heat detection machines with all the special handling that these entail, to scan deep inside an engine and search for faults before they become visible to the naked eye. Some of this equipment is portable in case there is a problem away from base.

Many major airlines carry out maintenance under contract for other airlines – sometimes even rivals. Airline lore tells the story of engineers who had finished a job on a rival's plane, and were found polishing it up by hand 'just to impress the others'.

Development engineers

Engineering staff play a much more important role in airlines than is generally recognized. As well as the 'normal' role of servicing and looking after engines, there are specialists who look after everything from electrics to seats. Development engineers are an elite corps within an engineering department, but they have an important role to play.

Case Study

The development engineer.

Airline seats are a precision engineering job, and whenever an airline decides to change its seats, development engineers will be given the task of coming up with something better than anything a rival can offer. No small task, when you know that rival airlines have teams doing exactly the same thing. The airline sets up a small team from marketing, purchasing and operations. Working as part of the development team with the engineers, they spend months going through every possibility – the seat must be fire-proof to a certain rating, light, and easy to install anywhere where the airline has a depot. Working with ergonomists they will try to make the seat as comfortable as possible for every type of passenger.

They also work with the IFE (in-flight entertainment) people to ensure that the latest gizmos can be incorporated into seats (there is enough hardware underneath each seat to run a powerful PC) and that wiring is easy to replace when something goes wrong. Recently, a plane returning from Asia with an English football team on board had its seats trashed – and the airline couldn't sell those seats until the plane returned to its base and the engineering department could fit replacements. The result was a huge loss of revenue for the airline, and back to the drawing board to try and make seats non-trashable by football teams and others.

Salary

With seats costing anything from £1,000 in economy to upwards of £5,000 in premium class, cost analysis is an important job. A recent BA ad for an engineering cost analyst to produce monthly schedules and cost summaries, and liaise with customers, offered a salary of £12,500 pa.

Airport maintenance

Airports also need engineers. Maintenance managers work in a challenging environment, developing airport maintenance, taking responsibility for the team overseeing day-to-day maintenance, and devising and implementing new ways to improve systems. Prospectives must have an HNC in an appropriate engineering discipline or have equivalent experience. Experience of introducing computerized maintenance procedures would be helpful.

Salary

Recent jobs advertised by the BAA included maintenance managers and technicians for Stansted Airport. Salaries ranged from £20,000 to £30,000 plus performance-related bonuses (Jan 2001). The ads stated that due to internal promotions the authority was looking for skilled technicians, dealing with everything from ground lighting to X-ray equipment. HNC or ONC qualified with a high level of mechanical and electrical expertise on plant and equipment and their associated control systems. Shift work 24 hours a day, 365 days a year.

Flight engineers

These work on the flight deck of aircraft, but, as Margaret Pecnik of BALPA says, 'this is a sunset career'. Aircraft are theoretically easier to fly today, and companies would prefer to employ two rather than three crew on a flight deck, so the flight engineer's job is being phased out. F/Es still work on RAF planes and for some freight airlines – and Concorde.

Helicopter engineers

The British Helicopter Advisory Board's Web site (www. bhab.demon.co.uk) has a training section with information: 'I want to be a helicopter engineer'.

Qualifications and training

To be selected for an apprentice scheme, school-leavers need a good education with GCSEs or A Levels (or equivalents) in Maths, English and Science. Once on the scheme, you select if you want to specialize in engines, airframes or aviation electronics. Most airlines now operate an attainment–based scheme – so you progress upwards every time you master a process, rather than waiting until you have served a certain time. Usually you work three–four years as an apprentice. Once this is finished, you then go on to specialized training. After approximately five years you obtain your licence and can sign for work you have carried out. When you sign, you are legally responsible for that work.

As an alternative to university, for those aged 18–24 with A Levels, BA runs an LAEs (Licensed Aircraft Engineers) programme. Over four years you combine working on the latest commercial aircraft with studies for an HND in Aeronautical Engineering Maintenance Licence, with the opportunity to go on to a BEng (Hons) in Air Transport Engineering.

Undergraduates interested in an industrial placement year with an engineering focus are based within the supply chain business (involved with companies that provide the products and spares that go into aircraft). Graduate engineers are recruited directly into engineering departments, maintenance and powerplant.

Case Study

Tom, an engineer, works at Heathrow.

Tom was always fascinated with engines; he financed a gap-year trip round the world by restoring and then selling a classic car. So when the offer of an apprenticeship for BA at Heathrow came up, he leapt at this.

'In your first year you study for your HND in Aeronautical Engineering and start studying for your JAR (Joint Airworthiness Requirement) 66 Licence. You also get hands-on experience. The next year you complete your HND and practice troubleshooting in BA's ground-based simulators. You also decide if you want to study for the BEng (Hons) in Transport Engineering (this will take extra time, reverting back to the programme for the final two years).'

During the third year 'You are assigned to a fleet or aircraft type to gain experience. Finally your last year is structured training in an operational environment and you sit your exams.' After four years he gets JAR 66 B1 and B2 Licences and an HND. After six years it is a degree. Now he is qualified, Tom works at Heathrow, but often flies abroad when an aircraft goes u/s away from base.

How to apply

Engineers are expected to be computer-literate, so many airlines initially ask you to fill in a form online. If your form fits, you will be invited for an assessment of classroom-based tests and group exercises with working engineers. You could then be invited back for a further interview.

Eligibility

You must have the right to live where the airline's engineering base is. You must be aged 18–24 for most British airlines and have or be expected to gain A Level Maths and Physics or a related Science subject, plus GCSEs or equivalent at Grade C in English and Maths.

8 Support services

An international airport is like a miniature city, with everything from a chapel to its own police force and fire brigade. The BAA employs over 500 fire-fighters, and every airport needs a small army of people doing different and exciting jobs.

Air traffic services

Air traffic control

A UK Civil Aviation Authority (CAA) Air Traffic Controllers Licence and a Meteorological Observers Certificate are needed for work at air traffic control. To obtain these you have to be trained at a CAA Airport.

You have to 'think in 3D' as you handle aircraft flying into your sector from different directions and at different levels. Work covers air traffic services, navigation, meteorology, telecommunications, aerodynamics, automatic data processing, etc. Training takes around three years, then you start as an air traffic control assistant supporting the controllers with visual control of the airfield both on the ground and in the air. Assistants respond to telephone and radio enquiries, provide meteorological and flight planning information and relevant air traffic information to other departments, and maintain the air traffic control tower diary and training records.

Competition is fierce. Aged 18–26, you need at least five

GCSEs or equivalent at Grade C or above, including Maths and English, and be able to work shifts, to even start on the career path for this demanding job. More information may be found on the Web site www.nats.co.uk.

The CAA has a Cadet Entry Scheme for candidates aged 18–26 with at least two A Levels (or equivalent) or three GCSE higher grades including Maths or a Science. Cadets are selected by tests and interviews. Or you may be able to obtain sponsorship, or pay for the course yourself.

Flight briefing

Flight briefing is part of the air traffic services department, providing flight-briefing services to aircrew in accordance with CAA regulations. This covers information on the telephone and personal enquiries, updating meteorological charts and information to visiting crews, flight-planning information, regularly updating the airport's computerized aircraft billing system (every time a plane lands it has to pay a fee), and processing payment of aircraft landing fees. For this, you will need GCSEs or equivalent in English, Maths, Geography and probably Physics.

Case Study

Eurocontrol *operates the Upper Area Control Centre at Beek in the Netherlands.*

Eurocontrol looks for students 18–25 with advanced secondary education who are medically fit (the application form includes an official certificate, which you have to take to an optician to fill out). You must have normal colour perception, good spoken and written English, and be a national of a Eurocontrol member state (EU, other European countries, and border countries including Moldova, Malta, Cyprus and Turkey).

You go through a rigorous testing process, which includes 'dynamic aptitude tests', and sign an undertaking to serve for at least four years with the agency. Documents are checked for criminal record history, if any, and you must be security cleared by your country.

Air Traffic Control at Eurocontrol generally works four days on and two days off. Depending on how busy are traffic patterns you could work 0800–1345; or 1340–2235; or 0830–1745 (filling in) or 2200–0800 (if at a major airport that is less busy at night-time).

Career progression can lead to positions as an instructor, or in training, research and development or operations. You cease active work at 55 or 57, and receive a pension.

Once you have experience, the Royal Air Force occasionally recruits aviation officers grade 2 (air traffic controllers) to be employed within the Civil Service, and commissioned in the RAF Reserve.

Car hire concessions

Most major car hire companies have desks at airports needing staff to work shifts, who are able to drive, with good customer service skills.

Catering

Most airlines today out-source their catering, and airlines buy meals from companies such as Alpha (who cater for 370,000 flights a year), Chelsea Catering (an American company), Cara (Canadian) and Gate Gourmet.

Case Study

Gate Gourmet.

When the IFCA (In-flight Catering Association) Conference was held in Gate Gourmet's home town of Geneva, the company went all out to capture catering contracts from those of the world's airlines attending this event.

Twelve hundred guests were entertained in a massive hanger at Geneva Airport. As they arrived, Cirque du Soleil entertainers greeted them, before they sat down to a six-course dinner prepared by 120 chefs working in a field kitchen. The final course was a 'Swiss Surprise'. Each guest was presented with a plate on which were six tiny frozen desserts (all different) and six piping hot puddings. To do this the chefs had prepared the plates that afternoon with the six frozen desserts, then stored them in portable freezers. Came the time for service, and all 120 chefs were waiting – as waiters came by with the frozen plates each chef popped on a tiny hot pudding – once past a brigade of six chefs the waiters came out to present the plates to the guests.

The result of this was orders for Gate Gourmet, including British Airways!

Foreign exchange cashiers

Most passengers will want to change money and they will look for a bureau de change at an airport. International Currency Exchange plc employs staff at airports around the world with outlets from Edinburgh to US airports. Staff are 18+, with good customer service skills, numerate, accurate, responsible and reliable. Ideally, you will have a banking or retail background, or be used to handling money.

IATA

Founded in 1919, IATA (International Air Transport Association) is the worldwide voice of around 270 of the world's airlines, flying over 95 per cent of all international scheduled air traffic. IATA talks directly to governments on airline matters.

Thanks to IATA, passengers can make one ticket booking and travel around the world on different airlines. Continual efforts by IATA ensure that people, freight and mail can fly easily around the world and members' aircraft can operate safely, securely, efficiently and economically under clearly defined rules. Before an airline is accepted into membership, it has to satisfy strict safety criteria. By monitoring and controlling airline costs, IATA helps keep down ticket prices.

Using IATA as a clearing house, members can settle credits and debits between themselves at one location. Last year more than 54,000 passenger agent offices sent $110 billion to more than 340 airlines using IATA's Billing and Settlement Plans.

For a travel agent to become accredited to IATA, it has to demonstrate financial soundness, have well-trained staff and have suitable secure premises to safeguard stocks of airline tickets. Airline tickets are almost as negotiable as currency, so they have to be kept under lock and key.

Another aspect of IATA's work is establishing standards for different airline services, such as special menus or facilities for disabled passengers. If you are diabetic, or need a vegetarian or any other special meal, thanks to IATA you can choose from 28 different menu categories recognized by airline caterers around the world. On the cargo side, its dangerous goods regulations set the standard, and its in-house publication, *Dangerous Goods Regulations*, is an unexpected bestseller!

When airlines want to start a new service, they have to bid for 'slots' to fly their aircraft into airports. IATA provides a forum between members who may have vested interests, governments and airports. Another service is fraud prevention. Currently stolen tickets cost the industry around £120 million a year, but IATA trains agents to recognize and prevent this. And good news for passengers who lose their luggage: IATA has formulated the Montreal Convention to replace the outdated Warsaw Convention with its pathetically low compensation payments. Hopefully, it will be ratified soon. Even better news: IATA is working on a safety programme to cut accident rates in half by 2004 compared with 1995.

All this work needs staff – and with offices in Montreal, Geneva, Amman, Beijing, Brussels, Dakar, London (Hounslow), Miami, Nairobi, Santiago de Chile, Singapore and Washington, DC, there should be something in most regions.

9 Shopping – the key to a profitable airport

A career in airport retailing can take you around the world. Every major airport relies heavily on airport shops for its revenue, and when duty-free privileges were abolished between EU states, many airports talked of increasing landing fees to make up the shortfall in revenue.

History

It all started 50 years ago, when Ireland's Shannon Airport wanted to increase income. To do this, it needed to encourage more planes to land. In those days, aeroplanes couldn't fly the Atlantic in one hop from major European airports, but had to refuel on their way to the United States. Shannon was ideally placed, but so were other airports. So the Shannon authorities came up with their USP (unique selling point) and opened the world's first duty-free airport shop. Soon passengers were booking on the airlines that refuelled at Shannon, so they could buy Irish crystal, spirits and other items duty free.

It wasn't long before other airports copied Shannon. When airport operators such as the British Airports Authority (BAA) realized they could earn as much or more from the retail side as from landing and take-off fees, retailing became big business. Major airport retailers are massive global companies, and the BAA has one of the best records in this field, leading Aer Rianta

(Eire), Gebr Heinemann (Germany), Nuance, etc. The BAA's company, World Duty Free, is so efficient that in the United States its airport retail operations earn more per US traveller than rival American companies.

The only blip came with the abolition of intra-Europe duty free in 1999. The European Union wants harmonization of laws across Europe – and regarded duty free as an anomaly disturbing this. After years of deliberation, and even though studies proved that abolition of duty free would actually cost jobs and money, one country – Denmark – voted to abolish duty free. Fourteen countries (including Britain) voted to keep the privilege, but because one country had voted for abolition, Brussels said it had to be abolished.

In the aftermath, retail operators did everything they could to make up for the loss; margins were squeezed to give passengers prices lower than their high-street price, bulk purchases kept prices low, and in the final analysis, when an airport like Heathrow has 50 per cent leisure (holiday) traffic, people going on holiday want to spend – currently an average of £3.81 for every passenger. Passengers travelling to destinations outside the EU can still buy duty free. Even though recently there was a downturn in traffic due to terrorism and foot-and-mouth disease, the BAA has made airport shopping so popular that it announced retail income was up 9 per cent, probably due in part to 'arrivals' stores – where passengers order goods on their way out, and pick them up on their return.

Where once the duty-free shop was hidden away in a dark corner, today when designing airports architects produce glitzy shopping malls. Some cynics say that aircraft delays happen so passengers have time to spend more. Whatever – delays keep the tills ringing merrily.

Employers

Retail

Retail shops operate landside (newsagents, chemists, etc) and airside in the duty-free area. Operators such as the BAA and its company World Duty Free are mega-employers, as is Nuance. These companies need thousands of staff to operate shifts around the clock, at airports around the world.

However, it's not just a case of serving behind a counter – currently Nuance is looking for staff in finance, business development, product management, marketing, logistics, IT, and of course sales. With outlets from Australia to Canada, and operating the Olympic concession at Athens Airport ready for the Games in 2004, Nuance is snapping at BAA's heels.

Most staff will start on sales, but if you are ambitious you will soon become a consultant – an advisor rather than sales staff. You have to be able to understand trends and marketing strategies. Clients are often 'time poor, cash rich' businesspeople, who will buy six month's supply of their favourite products in one go, or airline staff buying products to protect their skins (see Chapter 4).

Most cosmetic houses at airports are from the upper, luxury end. It doesn't make sense to pay massive franchise and rental charges to sell cheap skincare. Customers tend to go for more luxurious products if they think they are saving tax or duty. A company such as La Prairie will launch a cream costing £200 for a small jar, knowing there is a market for this at an airport. As Carole at Geneva says, 'You see them walking past taking a good look at our products, then coming up to us with a long shopping list headed by Skin Caviar Luxe Cream – sometimes three or four jars for friends who have heard how good it is, and want to save money buying this at the airport.' Impulse buying takes place amongst the fragrances, but skincare staff really have to know their products as customers ask detailed, in-depth questions.

Tip!

If you work in the main sales areas of duty free, you may have to sell alcohol, unless you are working in a country that forbids its sale. If you don't want to do this, then you need to work for one of the cosmetic or clothing franchises.

Skincare and cosmetics

There are small individual outlets such as Funky Fingers at Gatwick that need manicurists not only to provide traditional manicures, but also to apply temporary tattoos and nail art. The concession is operated by United Beauty, telephone 01773 536934. At the other end of the scale, large franchises such as Clarins need a big rota of staff not only for their retail side with numerous outlets, but also to provide massages, beauty treatments, tanning and facials at their airport studios. In between there are individual concessions such as Dior, Lancome, Helena Rubinstein, MAC, La Prairie and many others.

Chanel must have one of the oldest and best-known logos, and its skincare brands make full use of the striking black and white colours first chosen by Madame Chanel. Building on today's rush-rush, Chanel cleverly offers 'express treatments', in black-and-white plastic tubes with a toning and firming mask being marketed as Masque Lift Express, aimed at women whose skin is suffering from the effects of jet lag and stress.

Fragrances

Buying perfume goes with duty-free shopping. It costs literally millions to launch a new perfume, but with the huge turnover at airports, Chanel felt duty-free sales made it worthwhile to launch a special version of its classic perfume Chanel No 5. Aimed at travellers, it has a spray bottle and two refills, and is now a best-seller. For some, the only time they buy perfume is at the airport; others buy bottles for gifts, and sales staff need to be able to swing between the savvy shopper and the 'first time' mouse. Those perfume houses that only offer perfumes and eau de toilette (a diluted version of perfume) generally employ the staff who work for the airport retail operators. For companies such as Chanel, Dior, Estée Lauder, etc, which sell cosmetics as well as perfume, high sales volume makes it worthwhile employing their own staff.

Working conditions

Be prepared to work shifts. Many airports operate 24 hours around the clock, and 3 am can be as busy as 3 pm. You have to work fast – people are always in a hurry to catch their plane. Languages are useful, and you will be trained to identify cultural differences to help people make their choices when buying.

Although you may work just for one company, you cannot be there all the time. You form a working relationship with another consultant, so you understand and know each other's products. When you go for your break, your colleague takes over – even though he or she may be working for a rival house.

To familiarize you with the products, you will often be taken to the company's head office for training, which could be in Paris for Clarins or Chanel, or Switzerland for La Prairie. Sadly, the Japanese companies tend to bring their top staff, including chemists, over to Europe for staff training! You will be paid to fly over to these courses, and put up in top hotels. But the trip is not a holiday; it is hard but interesting work!

Salary

Rewards are good. Starting salaries are around £10,000 pa, but you can soon work up to £15,000–25,000. Managerial positions pay very well indeed. Benefits often include bonus schemes, subsidized meals, free life assurance and discounts. The major retailing companies operate duty-free outlets in the USA, Australia, Asia and all over the world, so if you like the work, there are opportunities to work in other countries.

Tip!

Recently Nuance was bought out by the Italian company PAM, which may mean opportunities to transfer between its Italian, Swiss and Hong Kong operations.

Case Study

Clarins operates beauty studios at Heathrow and Gatwick.

Facing the main area are sales counters, selling all Clarins products for men and women. Most of its products are fragrance-free, since the company discovered that men were buying them to counteract the effects of travel on their skin. Airport retail space is extremely expensive, so a treatment studio is cunningly designed to fit into the smallest space possible at the back of the counter. There, stressed travellers (male and female) have massages, facials and treatments. The difference between treatments here and ones in a normal beauty salon is that instead of taking an hour or 90 minutes, all treatments are geared to take 45 minutes (the optimum time for the average traveller).

Sally Morante works in the Clarins Gatwick studio. For some years, she worked for a well-known local salon, until deciding that shift work fitted in better with her lifestyle. She works quickly and efficiently to ensure that clients don't miss their plane, but has a soothing manner that makes you feel you don't care if you do! One of Sally's most popular treatments is an instant tanning session. Holidaymakers who want to look tanned, but don't want to risk exposure to the sun, book in for an exfoliating and tanning treatment with products that dry within one minute.

Whilst Sally is treating customers, she will also give them a gentle sales pitch, describing the treatment and what products she uses. At each step she took, she quietly told me what she was doing (reassuring) and what she was using (so I got the subtle message). She told me that she was using a Hydra balance cream and lotion designed for dehydration, which was good for frequent flyers. This made sense, so I came out and bought the product to continue the treatment whilst on holiday.

As I came out, feeling a million dollars, there was a carefully angled display shelf with tonic bath and relax bath lotions; Sally's colleague explained that the first was good for anti-stress, and the relax bath would help me sleep if suffering from jet lag. The end result was a feeling of well-being, and the effective training each staff member takes makes customers feel they have made a choice to buy products that will do them good, and fit in with their lifestyle.

Finding work

If you like a certain perfume house, phone its head office and ask if it is recruiting. Phone your local airport or look on its

Web site; click on shopping and apply to the concessionaire. Look out for ads in local papers. Ask at the jobcentre.

Tip!

Even if you aren't working in the retail section, don't forget that you can take advantage of often-lower prices at the airport, especially if you want IT equipment. BAA has pioneered a scheme whereby, provided you are travelling, you can buy this and have it delivered to your home – phone 0800 844 844 for more details.

---

10 Customs and Excise and immigration

Customs and Excise

Customs and Excise is a national organization with offices all over the United Kingdom, employing around 23,000. It also has links with customs services abroad and works closely with colleagues in the EU. While the fight against drug trafficking and other illegal trade is highest priority, it is primarily concerned with gathering revenue from a variety of sources: value added tax (VAT), customs duties (on goods entering the country) and excise duties (on goods like petrol, alcohol and tobacco). In total, C & E collects 40 per cent of central government taxation every year.

History

Customs and Excise is probably the oldest of our government 'forces', dating back to at least 743. By the 13th century there was a national organization of customs service, and when you declare something you bought abroad, the customs officer looks up duty payable in a book of rates, first published in 1506.

As a temporary measure to pay for the Civil War, excise duty was levied on beer in 1643 – and it is still there today. At the same time, duty was levied on spirits. This was incredibly unpopular and helped 'glamourize' smuggling. When gin, whisky, etc were regarded as social drinks, the average person thought nothing of trying to evade duty. Kipling wrote in a poem 'watch the wall, my darling, whilst the gentlemen ride by', meaning smugglers carrying 'brandy to the parson, baccy (tobacco) to the clerk' were people well-known in the community. People looked away so they could truthfully say they hadn't seen smuggled goods.

During the Napoleonic Wars smuggling was rife. When customs officers seized one cargo of lace the value was over a million pounds. Notorious highwaymen attacked customs officers, and at one time they couldn't ride out 'between dusk and dawn'.

Today, the fight is against more organized criminals, and carried out by computer rather than hand-to-hand fighting. But those working in the service are following in the footsteps of Geoffrey Chaucer and Robert Burns, both customs officials. If you want to learn more, visit the H.M. Customs and Excise National Museum in Liverpool.

Customs officers form the first line of defence against all forms of smuggling, and ensure that health and trade regulations are obeyed. However, the move towards the European Market means that fewer jobs are available than previously. Although it remains an important area of work, you are likely to start your career in the revenue-gathering section. There are opportunities for dog handlers with 'sniffer' detection dogs (anti-terrorist and drugs), but you have to be a serving officer before you can apply to join a dog-handling unit.

Entry requirements

Entry into Customs and Excise is by the civil service entry exam. IT skills are important, as much work is on projects worked out on computers. The higher the job band, the higher the pay. You will need:

♦ Job Bands 5/6: 5 GCSE passes or equivalent (including English Language), including 2 at A Level (or equivalent), generally aged 17–55;

- ◆ Job Bands 3/4: 5 GCSE or equivalent passes at Grade C (including English Language), generally aged 16–59;
- ◆ Job Bands 1/2: 2 GCSE or equivalent passes at Grade C (including English Language), generally 16–59.

Working conditions

Jobs are to be found all over Britain, at large and small airports. Work is varied, and not many people know these officers have the right to make arrests. For more information, ring 01702 367888 or see the Web site www.hmce.gov.uk.

Immigration

Working alongside Customs and Excise is Immigration. It is the Immigration team that asks to see your passport when you arrive at or leave an airport. The Immigration Service comes under the Home Office, and has two main functions. First, at ports of entry, it is responsible for the control of persons entering the country and decides whether to admit them. Where and when necessary, they refuse entry and supervise the removal of those who have entered or attempted to enter the country in breach of immigration laws.

Second, Immigration is responsible for identifying those already in the country who have no authority to remain, and removes them.

Duties include examination of passengers, surveillance and intelligence-based activity, forgery detection and the gathering of evidence. Officers in the enforcement field regularly conduct immigration visits with police assistance. Their aim is to provide a high-quality and non-discriminatory immigration control in accordance with the law, published service standards and the UK's international obligations.

Those words don't really tell you the overall picture. If you have an analytical and enquiring mind, and are happy with IT, then you could find work in this service fascinating. Find out more on www.homeoffice.gov.uk.

Entry requirements

Entry into a career in Immigration is by the Civil Service entry exam.

11 The interview

As soon as an airline receives your application/CV/letter, it will look at your experience and qualifications and check whether you have submitted all the information required. Leave anything out, and it's into the wpb with your application – so check, check and check again before you send off any form. Around 80 per cent of applicants receive a 'no' on the basis of their written application.

Telephone interviews

Sometimes you will be given a telephone interview before you even fill in an application form. So before you phone, think of the '60 second test'. In one minute summarize:

- Why do you want to work for the airline?
- Why do you think you will make a good team member?
- What experience have you had that fits you for working with the public?
- What skills can you bring to the airline if it employs you?

Don't go on too long – people talk themselves out of a job by talking too much.

Tip!

If the form doesn't arrive, you've failed. So phone again, but be better prepared.

Pre-interview

Good preparation is the way to overcome interview nerves. Familiarity breeds contentment in this case.

◆ Find out about the company – if it is a large company, phone the company secretary and ask for copy of the annual report.
◆ Look at its Web site (if it has one).
◆ Look at the *Telegraph, Times, Financial Times,* etc Web sites for info about the company, especially in the financial pages.
◆ Ask friends if they know anyone working for the company.
◆ Lay out clothes the night before.
◆ ALWAYS plan to arrive at least one hour in advance – you have that time spare if there is a hold-up.
◆ Check the address – the interview may not be held at company offices.
◆ Take a spare copy of your CV plus one for you to check what you have said.

If you have heard about horrendous interview techniques, you might like to know that the sadists who devised these are being told intimidation does not get the best out of a workforce. 'It's reassurance and confidence building that are the buzzwords today', according to Suzy Siddons, author of *Developing Your People*.

At the interview

Companies look for:

◆ a team worker;
◆ stamina;

- smart appearance;
- ability to 'think on your feet';
- good communication skills;
- customer service experience and experience of dealing with the public;
- common sense;
- good spoken and written English;
- literacy and numeracy;
- outgoing personality;
- enthusiasm and flexible approach.

Most airlines operate a 'group' interview, which can take a complete day and might include:

1. a welcome and introduction to the company;
2. a written test – short questions on literacy and numeracy;
3. a face-to-face interview in front of a panel;
4. group interaction and 'games'.

Check if the airline wants anything else, eg KLM uk asks you to give a short talk about yourself.

Tip!

Think of any charity work you have done, and make sure you mention this. At a recent interview in Liverpool, out of 300 applicants, every one of the 19 chosen had carried out some work for a charity.

Interview advice

During the day, the written test usually includes general knowledge questions. What are the capital cities of European countries, which countries are in the European Union, what is their currency? What is the name of the chairman of the airline for which you wish to work?

Don't know? Well start reading a quality newspaper every day and if you are on the Internet get into the habit of visiting the *Financial Times* and other financial news Web sites. You will be surprised at what you can find when you key in 'airline' or 'airport'. Read trade magazines (listed at the end of the book).

You will be tested on literacy and numeracy. This will include doing sums converting from one currency to another, so make sure you keep up to date with various European currencies and what they are worth. Look these up in the business section of a good newspaper. If you forget them, just say 'I looked this up in the *Telegraph* this morning, but I've forgotten...' Read through the questions several times – there are lots of trick questions. For example in the numeracy test, you may be asked to give equivalents for £2 not £1.

Dress smartly. This means a suit or jacket and trousers if you are male, and a tie (can be colourful but clean with no food stains!). Not too much jewellery; if in doubt leave it off. And no visible body piercing or tattoos.

Women should wear a suit, jacket and skirt or smart dress. If you are happier wearing a trouser suit, that is all right, but it must look business-like. Wear make-up, but nothing glittery; nails can have discreet nail polish but again nothing too flash. Not too much jewellery; if in doubt leave it off. No visible body piercing or tattoos. If you are wearing nail polish, take the bottle for touch-ups in case you chip a nail.

ALWAYS make sure your shoes are clean and polished. And no, trainers are not acceptable. Make sure nails are well groomed and clean (you would be surprised how many interviewers take a good look at your hands).

Tip!

If you have to wear a coat and/or carry an umbrella, make sure you leave this outside the interview room. Clutter drops around you.

You are going to feel nervous. The interview panel will be expecting this. They don't like cocky applicants who know it all, but will make allowances for nervousness. If you think you are making a bad impression, take a deep breath and start again.

Tip!

During the interview day a nice person may give you an amusing and interesting account of the history of the company. Most people relax and laugh when this happens. Pay attention! At the end of a tiring day, you will be given a paper asking you questions about what he or she told you. Sneaky!

For certain jobs, you will be tested on your reaction to stress: don't be frightened. In a recent survey, workers in stressful jobs showed that they are able to rest and relax when they need to; stress was seen as part of the job – which can get the adrenaline going.

What else will be covered?

If you haven't been interviewed before, a good interview panel will get you to relax by asking questions about your background, education, work experience, general career expectations, hobbies and leisure activities. Answer truthfully, but don't go on too long – your enthusiasm can take up too much of the panel's time, and you don't get a chance to answer other questions that might help your application.

So what happens if you have made a hash of the interview? That means you are human, and it is often what interviews are all about. The 'too perfect' candidate can actually get up an interviewer's nose; they expect you to be worried and nervous, and if you aren't, or come over as too cocky, you will be turned down. 'Team players' are what are wanted, not individuals who want the boss's job – that comes once you are working!

If you are not successful, use the interview experience, apply to other airlines, and keep on. Or apply again – often the same airline will accept you if you are a year older. Time and time again when interviewing people for this book, they said that they had been turned down – some several times. Be persistent!

Tip!

Beware – one well-known airline will ask you at the end of a long day to try on its uniform. If you are female you will also receive a complete make-up. You think all this attention means you have the job. WRONG. It is to see if you look good in the uniform. If your skin clashes with its bright house colours, then it is No-No.

What happens if you are successful at interview? Well Done! You now go on the appropriate training or induction course at the start of your career! GOOD LUCK!

12 Useful contacts and information

Books

If you can't find these books in shops, most publishers operate a telephone hotline for credit card orders, but remember their charge will probably include postage.

Brown, G A *Airline Passenger's Guerrilla Handbook*, Blakes Publishing. On the desk of one of the industry's top lawyers, and lots of savvy travellers. Gives 'other' side of the industry – a good read and very informative. $14.95. ISBN 0-924022-04-3.

Careers in the Travel Industry, Kogan Page. £8.99. ISBN 0-7494-1820-6.

Corfield, R *Preparing Your Own CV*, Kogan Page. £7.99. ISBN 0-7494-2852-X.

Reed A *Airline – The Inside Story of British Airways*, BBC Books. Gives an excellent insight into the workings of an airline. ISBN 00563-20718-3.

'Working in Tourism', *Vacation Work*. £9.99. ISBN 1 85458 133 3. Tel: (01865) 241978.

Grants

Ask your local education authority for a copy of *Grants to*

Students: A Brief Guide. If you are unable to obtain a grant, there are career development loans, which are government-funded loans for training. They have to be repaid, but at favourable rates, and often not until you have started earning. Tel: 0800 585 505.

Magazines

Airline Business   Tel: 020 8652 4996
Airline World   Tel: 01628 604311
Airports International   Tel: 01892 784099
Careerscope   Tel: 01276 21188
Flight International   www.flight.international.co.uk
Helicopter World   Tel: 01628 604311
In-Flight (UK)   Tel: 01628 604311
In-Flight (USA)   www.inflightusa.com
International Flight Training News   www.iftn.co.uk
Pilot Magazine   www.pilotmagazine.com
Regional Airline World   Tel: 01628 604311

Other useful contacts

Air League
Broadway House
Tothill Street
London SW1H 9NS
Tel: 020 7222 8463
www.airleague.co.uk
Offers specific advice to individuals in response to their queries. Careers advice is free of charge on flying@airleague.co.uk.

ATA (Aviation Training Association)
Dralda House
Crendon Street
High Wycombe HP13 6LS
www.aviation-training.org
This charity is a focal point for training standards in the industry. Information pack about Cabin Crew Training (small charge).

BAA (British Airports Authority)
Tel: 0845 60 60 234
www.baa.co.uk
BAA Shopping Information Line
Tel: 0800 844 844

BALPA (British Airline Licensed Pilots' Association)
With over 7,000 members, it is the largest Flight Crew Association for pilots and flight engineers outside the USA. It says membership 'enchances careers and lifestyle', and if you are starting a pilot's training course you are entitled to a year's free membership. Visit its Web site www.balpa.org for info on becoming a pilot.

Bournemouth and Poole College
North Road
Parkstone
Poole BH14 OL9
Tel: 01202 747600
Offers the new Air Cabin Crew Vocational Qualification.

CAA (Civil Aviation Authority)
CAA House
Room T516
Kingsway
London WC2B 6TE
Tel: 020 7379 7311
It is responsible for granting of pilot, flight engineer and radio-telephony licences and qualifications for aeroplanes, helicopters and gyroplanes, airships and 'free' balloons.

Cabair College of Air Training
Cranfield Airport
Bedford MK43 OJR
Tel: 01234 751243
www.ccat.org.uk
Commercial Pilot Training. Occasionally runs part-sponsored training on behalf of British European Airlines, KLM uk, etc.

Career Development Loans
Tel: 0800 585 505

Customs and Excise
www.hmce.gov.uk

Eurocontrol
(European Organization for the Safety of Air Navigation)
Rue de la Fusee 96
B-1130 Brussels.
Tel: 00 31 43 366 1234 Fax: 00 32 2 729 9070
www.eurocontrol.be

IAPA (International Air Passengers' Association)
Main objective is to reach 'zero' flight accident level. The Association actively promotes continued study and assessment of factors that may affect accident rates, etc, such as: pilot training; aircraft engineering and configuration improvements; cabin safety and evacuation concepts; effective air traffic control.
Membership details: www.iapa.com

IATA (International Air Transport Association)
Head Office
800, Place Victoria
Montreal
Quebec
Canada H4Z 1M1

European Office
33, Route de l'Aéroport
1215 Geneva 15 Airport
Switzerland

London Office
Central House
Lampton Road
Hounslow
Middx TW3 1HY
Tel: 020 8607 6200
www.iata.org

Institute of Logistics and Transport
Tel: 01536 740100
www.iolt.org. uk
(formerly Chartered Institute of Transport)

North Lindsey College
Scunthorpe
Tel: 01724 291111
Offers the new Air Cabin Crew Vocational Qualification.

Nuance Airport Retail
Tel: 00 41 1 1874 39 46
www.nuancegroup.com

Pan Aviation Training services
Tel: 01293 862316
panaviation@yahoo.com
Develops qualifications for the industry. Courses include Air
Cabin Crew Vocational Qualification; Passenger Handling
NVQ Levels 2 and 3; Foundation for Modern Apprenticeship
in Aviation.

Plymouth College of FE
Tel: 01752 305700
www.pcfe.ac.uk
Offers the new Air Cabin Crew Vocational Qualification.

Simplifying Passenger Travel
A joint initiative among passenger airlines, airports, control
authorities and technology suppliers to improve passenger

satisfaction. www.simplifying-travel.org tells you about future developments.

Tourism Training Organization
Premium Rate Helpline (£1 per minute) 0906 553 2056 with advice on interviews, which airlines are recruiting, help with filling in forms, etc.

Travel Training Company
Tel: 01483 727321
www.ttctraining.co.uk

13 Company addresses

Some companies like you to send in a postcard or letter with an sae for their application form. Others expect you to telephone, or visit their Web site and download an application form. The appropriate method of contact is listed below.

Most airlines need both ground staff such as PSAs, and cabin crew. Generally, cabin crew and pilots will be based at an airline's base. But wherever an airline flies to, it will need local ground handling staff. Sometimes it employs its own staff locally, at other times airlines use local ground handling companies.

Aerolineas Argentinas
Bouchard 547
9th Floor
Buenos Aires 1106
Argentina

Air 2000
www.air2000.com
Cabin Crew Recruitment
7th Floor
Commonwealth House
Chicago Avenue
Manchester Airport M90 3DP for Gatwick base.

Air New Zealand International
www.airnewzealand.co.nz
Employs London-based flight attendants to operate London–Los Angeles–London routes. Applications on official application form from:
Phoenix Resourcing Services and Management Technology
Delta House
175 Borough High Street
SE1 1XP
Tel: 020 7939 9947

Airtours International
Parkway Three
Parkway Business Centre
300 Princess Road
Manchester B14 7LU
Admin, Personnel: Tel: 0161 232 6637, Cabin Crew Tel: 0161 232 6878

Air Traffic Control
Tel: 020 7832 5413/5555
www.nats.co.uk/recruitment

Airworld
Cabin Crew Recruitment
Room 102
Bristol Airport BS19 3DY
Crew based at Bristol, Cardiff, Gatwick and Manchester.

Aviation Job Search
www.aviationjobsearch.com
a Web site with details of jobs, training courses and who is hiring whom.

Avis
Send CV and covering letter to avis@corporateresearchltd.com
Tel: 01274 862 999

bmi (British Midland)
Donington Hall
Castle Donington DE74 2SB
Tel: 01332 854990
or
BM Training Centre
Stockley Close
West Drayton UB7 9BL
or e-mail CV to cabincrew.recruitment@flybmi.com

Britannia Airways
London Luton Airport
Luton LU2 9ND
e-mail: webjobs@uk.britaniaairways.com
19+ Luton and Stansted. World's largest charter airline.

British Airways
PO Box 10
London Heathrow Airport
Hounslow TW6 2JA
www.britishairwaysjobs.com
Air Cabin Crew Tel: 020 8940 2777, Trainee Pilots Tel: 0870
607 3777, Engineering, Administration, IT, Industrial Place-
ments, Graduates, Tel: 0870 60 80 747
or
PO Box 59
Heathrow Airport TW6 2SL
or
e-mail your CV to hr.1.recruitment@britishairways.com

British European
www.british-european.com
Vacancies posted on Web site.

Brymon Airways
Meridian
Worle Parkway
Weston-super-Mare BS22 6WA
Tel: 0870 2420033
www.brymon.com recruitment@brymon.com

Buzz
Endeavour House
Stansted Airport, CM24 1RS
English + European language. Based at Stansted. Send CV + full length photo to KLM Recruitment www.buzzaway.com

Cathay Pacific
www.cathaypacific.com/careers
Unless they mention nationality, all jobs at Cathay are open to any applicant from around the world.

City College Norwich
Tel: 01603 773311
information@cnn/ac.uk

Customs and Excise
21 Victoria Avenue
Southend-on-Sea SS99 1AA
Tel: 01702 367888
Apply to your local international airport, or send postcard for application form to above address.

EasyJet
Tel: 01582 525484
www.easyJet.com
Bases at Liverpool, Luton, Gatwick, Glasgow, Edinburgh, Geneva, Schiphol. They are honest about admitting that although Cabin Crew don't serve meals, they have to sell refreshments, and clean the cabin in between flights. It was this company that featured in the documentary *Airline*, so obviously, if working as a PSA you have to be able to follow the company line when dealing with passengers.

Emirates
95 Cromwell Road
London SW7 4DL
Cabin Crew are based in Dubai. Send CV and covering letter in
English, stating height and weight, together with one full length
and one passport-sized photo in colour to Recruitment.

Euroscot Express
Tel: 087 06070809
Flies out of Bournemouth and Glasgow.

Excalibur Airways
East Midlands Airport
Castle Donington DE74 2SA

GB Airways
Personnel Manager
GB Airways
The Beehive
Gatwick Airport, RH6 0LA

GO
Recruitment Office
2nd Floor
Enterprise House
Stansted Airport, CM24 1SB
www.gofly.com

Hertz
Human Resources
34 Staines Road
Hounslow, TW3 3LZ

Immigration
www.homeoffice.gov.uk

International Currency Exchange
Head of Personnel
47 Piccadilly
London W1J OLR
www.iceplc.com

JAL (Japanese Airlines)
Cabin Crew Dept
D'Albiac House
Cromer Road
London Heathrow Airport
Hounslow TW6 1NP
www.jal.co.uk

JMC
Gatwick, Manchester, Bristol, Cardiff, Glasgow, Luton,
Newcastle or Stansted. Information pack and application form:
Manchester Tel: 0161 489 0646.

KLM uk
Recruitment Co-ordinator
Endeavour House
Stansted Airport, CFM24 1RS
PSAs at Aberdeen, Birmingham, Edinburgh, Glasgow, Humber-
side, Leeds/Bradford, Manchester, Newcastle, Norwich and
Stansted. They have a pre-recorded recruitment information
line on 01279 660402.

Lauda Air
www.laudair.com
Austrian Charter Airline. German speakers.

Lufthansa
www.lufthansa.com
German-speaking staff. Log on to Career Lounge on Web site.

Meridiana
Zona Industriale A
Olbia (SS) 07026
Italy
www.meridiana.it
Its motto is 'Your Private Airline' and the smart, well-dressed
Cabin Crew give the impression you are flying with a superior
airline.

Monarch Airlines
Cabin Crew Recruitment
London Luton Airport
Luton
Beds LU2 9ND
Cabin Crew: www.monarch-airlines.com
Fluency in certain European languages or nursing qualifications
qualifies for extra payment. Tel: 01582 400000. No e-mail
applications.

Norwich Airport
Personnel Dept
Norwich Airport Ltd
Amsterdam Way
Norwich NR6 6JA
Tel: 01603 420678
personnel@norwichairport.com

Olympic Airways
HR Dept
100, Syngrou Avenue
Athens
Greece
www.olympic-airways.com
Greek speaking.

Qatar Airways
MBM Recruitment
Mead House
Church Lane Ewshot
Farnham GU10 5BJ
Based at Doha in the Gulf. Cabin Crew aged 20–30; good written and spoken English. In covering letter explain why you would like to work as Cabin Crew.

Royal Air Force
CS (M) 4b3
HQPTC
RAF Innsworth
Gloucester GL3 1EZ
Tel: 01452 712612 Ext 5091

Ryanair
Cabin Crew Recruitment
Dublin Airport
Ireland
Tel: 01279 666270
www.ryanair.com
Minimum age 18 for Cabin Crew.

SAS (Scandinavian Airlines System)
Fack
Stockholm S-195 87
Sweden
Flight Academy: www.sasfa.com
You have to speak English and Scandinavian languages.

Scot Airways
Tel: 0870 6060707
www.scoAirways.co.uk
Based at Cambridge Airport.

Servisair
FREEPOST NWW 13375
Bramhall
Cheshire SK7 2YF
Passenger Service Agents needed at Gatwick, Stansted and Manchester. Write to above address.

United Airlines
People Services
United House
South Perimeter Road
Heathrow Airport, TW6 3LP
www.unitedairlines.co.uk
Write enclosing CV to above address.

Virgin Atlantic Airways
2nd Floor
Ashdown House
High Street
Crawley RH10 1DQ
or Tel: 01293 747800 for application form.

World Duty Free
Room 236
Terminal 2 Office Block
Heathrow Airport
Hounslow TW6 1WD
Retail staff to work at airports.

Glossary

ABTA	Association of British Travel Agents
ADM	Airport Duty Manager
ATC	Air Traffic Control
ATOL	Air Travel Organizer's Licence
ATPL	Airline Transport Pilot's Licence
BAA	British Airports Authority
BALPA	British Air Line Pilots Association
bumped	When an airline is overbooked and there are not enough seats.
CAA	Civil Aviation Authority
CDL	Career Development Loan
CPL	Commercial Pilot's Licence
CSA	Customer Service Agents
DVT	Deep vein thrombosis
EDT	Estimated time of departure
IATA	International Air Transport Association
IFE	In-flight entertainment
IT	Information Technology

JAA	Joint Aviation Authority
JAR	Joint Airworthiness Requirement
LAE	Licensed Aircraft Engineer
leg	Journey section
pax	passengers
PPL	Private Pilot's Licence
slot	Timed allocation of landing or take-off rights at an airport.
stopover	Staying overnight/several nights away from base
TM	Terminal Manager
TTC	ABTA's Travel Training Company
u/s	Unserviceable – broken down.
VQ	Vocational (work) Qualification

Index